THE TRUTH WILL MAKE YOU FREE

The Truth
Will Make You Free

Rudolf Schnackenburg

HERDER AND HERDER

1966
HERDER AND HERDER NEW YORK
232 Madison Avenue, New York 10016

Original edition:
Von der Wahrheit die freimacht,
Munich, Anton Pustet KG, 1964.
Translated by Rodelinde Albrecht.

Nihil obstat: Brendan Lawlor
                Censor Deputatus
Imprimatur: † Robert F. Joyce
                Bishop of Burlington
                May 17, 1966

Library of Congress Catalog Card Number: 66–22611
© 1966 by Herder and Herder, Inc.
Manufactured in the United States

Foreword

I have the pleasure here of offering to the reading public three lectures which were originally delivered during Salzburg University Week in 1963. The central theme of that Week was "Truth in the Theological and Philosophical Context of Our Time," and I was asked to treat of "Sacred Scripture as the Present Revelation of Truth."

It seems that the biblical interpretation of truth which I then offered provided a number of liberating answers to many of the questions of my young university listeners, answers which they were very much concerned to know. I would be particularly pleased, therefore, should these lectures, now in book form, be read and studied by students, for whom the question of truth has become an abiding preoccupation.

The original papers have been altered only slightly, though I have enlarged them somewhat. In the original lectures, I ignored many topics which persons especially interested in exegesis and theology may have wanted to see treated, so for this reason I have added Chapter IV, "The Concept of Revelation in the Bible," an essay which I had published early in 1963 in *Biblische Zeitschrift,* and which I hope will shed some light on a few of their questions.

May this small work lead its reader to a greater appreciation of biblical revelation, and deepen his love and respect for the word of God.

R. S.

Contents

THE TRUTH WILL MAKE YOU FREE

I.

Truth as Divine Revelation

". . . and the truth will make you free" (Jn. 8, 32). This biblical phrase is often brought to mind and to bear by philosophers and scholars, by speakers and politicians, but it is seldom understood in its original meaning and grasped in its depth. The concept of truth has many facets and degrees of meaning. For the philosopher, there is a logical and ontological truth; for the historian, a historical truth; for the lawyer, the truth of testimony and evidence. But in our own time, in our scientific age, very often the only thing valued as true is that which has filtered through empirical investigation and scientific deduction, that which can be classified, which can be verified in an equation or rule or law, and which is thus for thinking men something no longer to be doubted. Truth becomes the correctness of observation, of the facts of the matter, of opinion, of deduction. However, though this reduced and limited concept of truth may perhaps satisfy scientific research, it cannot appease the longing of man for truth.

The truth of newly acquired expert knowledge might certainly be able to elevate man, but it cannot make him free from all those things which he perceives as narrowing and depressing. Man posits the question of truth not only for the sake of the matter which he is trying to penetrate intellectually, but also for his own sake, since he cannot in the same way as other things become the object of full and exact scientific investigation. He also wants to know the answer to such questions as "Who am I?", "Where did I come from and where am I going?", "What is the meaning of my existence?", "Can I even answer these questions?"

Here is where the Bible becomes the book of revelation, a book which can answer these questions about the existence of man, not by reason of human experiment which it records, but because it contains divine revelation. The Bible is concerned neither with philosophical knowledge nor with probing the question of the individual's existence, nor with a consideration of historical facts, nor with judging present conditions and political facts; rather, it is concerned with the religious truth, the question concerning the meaning of human existence, with the origin and goal of man, his course and behavior on earth, lastly with the question of salvation. Analogous to revelation, the self-disclosure of God himself, the Bible as the book of revelation provides in a decisive and authoritative way a clear answer to these questions. The relation of man to God as the foundation and goal of man's existence is for the Bible the only really important question. Through religion, man's bond with God, it gives the answer, and shows him the way to salvation.

However, because the Bible is written by men, in human language, there are a number of questions to be asked. How, for instance, is the divinely revealed truth contained in the Bible presented to us? Is this truth immediately "present"; is it recognizable, comprehensible, applicable, feasible in our existence? Is it always valid and definitive, and is it yet able to speak to us in *our own* time, answering the questions relative to *our own* spiritual state, *our own* historical situation, *our own* personal existence? Furthermore, what concrete form does the truth of biblical revelation take? How does the truth of revelation confront us in the Bible, in this book written by so many men down through so many centuries?

To answer these questions, therefore, we must begin by finding out what the Bible itself means by "truth."

1. THE CONCEPT OF "TRUTH" IN THE BIBLE

Even in a discussion of the biblical concept of truth, we are dealing with a word that has many meanings. Indeed, the chief characteristics of the Hebrew word *"emeth"* are "firmness" and "constancy," "dependability" and "fidelity." While the Greek word *"ἀλήθεια"* etymologically means "not to make secret," the Hebrew word, on the other hand, comes from the root-word "to stand firm," "to be constant." Thus the Greek word linguistically refers to the essence, while the Hebrew rendering is concerned more with the action, the behavior, the affairs of man. There is a striking rabbinical ex-

13

pression which states this Hebrew idea: "The world stands upon three things: upon justice, truth, and peace" (R. Simeon ben Gamaliel in *Mischna Aboth,* 1, 18). On the human level, "truth" in the Bible is in close relationship with lawful behavior: to speak justice in truth. The "words of peace and truth" of Est. 9, 30 validly attest to this fact. Everything is true which has and makes for a durable foundation, which guarantees dependability and certainty, which is permanent and valid. The Hebrew man did not seek to explore the world and its reasons for existence, but rather he sought to fashion his life according to just values.

In its religious sense, however, truth is plainly identified with God. It is on his word, order, and promise that one can unconditionally rely and build. ". . . thou art God, and thy words are true" (2 Sam. 7, 28). "For the word of the Lord is upright; and all his work is done in faithfulness" (Ps. 33, 4). Thus, in translating the biblical text, we are often hesitant in deciding whether to use "truth" or "faithfulness." In Neh. 9, 33 the Israelites acknowledge: "Yet thou hast been just in all that has come upon us, for thou hast dealt faithfully and we have acted wickedly." In Ps. 43, 3 the Psalmist entreats the Lord: "Oh send out thy light and thy truth [faithfulness]; let them lead me, let them bring me to thy holy hill and to thy dwelling." Because truth and fidelity come from God, "grace" and "truth" are frequently united in a double expression, which is best translated as "favor and faithfulness." God is a merciful and kind God, patient, rich

14

in favor and faithfulness (Ex. 34, 6). All the paths of the Lord are favor and fidelity for those who keep his covenant and commandments (Ps. 25, 10); grace and truth are before his countenance (Ps. 89, 15); they belong to his nature and his action. Israel is convinced that the grace and truth of God or his favor and fidelity rule over them eternally (Ps. 117, 2). One time he is directly named the "God of truth [faithfulness]" (Ps. 31, 5), and in the hands of this trustworthy God the devout person knows that he is safeguarded and redeemed. But the truth of God also demands of man that he love the truth and observe it, that he "do right by the truth," as the colloquial phrase has it. In the admonitions of old Tobit to his son we read these words: "For if you act truthfully, all your undertakings will be successful" (Tob. 4, 6). We find this mode of expression even now in the Qumrân texts, and we meet it a second time in the Johannine writings (Jn. 3, 21; 1 Jn. 1, 6). Truth is realized in moral action. Whoever "does right by the truth" comes to the Light, that is, Christ.

However, what man should do so that his ways are "true and just" is told him by God. In the Old Testament, God's will and truth were revealed to man in the Law (Torah): "He has showed you, O man, what is good; and what does the Lord require of you but to do justice, and to love kindness, and to walk humbly with your God?" (Mic. 6, 8). The members of the Qumrân community should "be perfect in everything which is revealed in the entire Torah in order to practice truth and righteousness, justice and true love, and to walk together in humility" (1 QS 8, 1f.). At the height of biblical revelation, namely, in the New Testament, "truth" is in substance determined by the saving message of Jesus Christ, the "Gospel." In the faith, one takes up the "word of truth" (see Eph. 1, 13; Col. 1, 5; etc.). St. Paul commends himself by "the open statement of the truth" (2 Cor. 4, 2); but this statement is above all made not as a teaching, but rather as the announcement of a reality, the reality of God's word, which brings salvation to men. The "truth of Christ" is in the Apostle (2 Cor. 11, 10); he can do nothing contrary to the truth, but only that which promotes the truth (2 Cor. 13, 8). In the word of proclamation truth confronts men, and they experience the grace of God (see Col. 1, 5f.). Thus, in the true spirit of faith, one must accept the truth, "obey" it (Gal. 5, 7), and "learn the Christ" in whom is the truth (see Eph. 4, 20f.). Divine truth is a message to mankind, a message of salvation, but also a challenge. It is not first of all a teaching about hidden things, but a demanding existential power which promises salvation to man only if he is willing to dispose himself to it. It is strongly empha- sized as an object of "knowledge" only in the pastoral letters against heresies; but this is no mere theoretical knowledge, rather it is the knowledge of faith which demands the deci- sion of one's entire being (see 2 Tim. 2, 25).

Truth appears in its most mature and profound sense, as the revealed word of God, in the Gospel of St. John, since it is here that its irremovable connection with the person of Christ is seen and demonstrated. The *Logos* made man is "full of grace and truth" (Jn. 1, 14), he speaks nothing except the truth (Jn. 8, 45f.), and everyone who "is of the truth" hears his voice (Jn. 18, 37). He, descended from heaven, has brought the truth "from above," from the divine realm unattainable to man, down to earth (see Jn. 3, 31–34), and reveals it in his words, in his "signs," in his very person. He *is* the truth (Jn. 14, 6), simply divine truth, and in everything that he says and does he bears witness to the truth. For that reason, because he is the life-giving truth, he is the way for men, the only way to the Father (Jn. 14, 6). It is not individual "truths" (the plural is never used) which Jesus Christ brings to light, but the indivisible divine truth which is in him and which he allows men to share. Only in the personalistic, Johannine, Christological concept of truth does truth in terms of divine revelation become complete and fully understandable. It is this truth, which "the Son" brings to us, which will make us free.

2. THE TRUTH DISCLOSED IN BIBLICAL REVELATION

After having considered the Bible's own testimony on what it understands "truth" to mean, it becomes easier for us to determine the relationship between biblical truth and the truth of human science; and we are also better enabled to

17

protect the "content of truth" of the Bible from false exegesis, and to discover its genuine meaning.

Natural Science and Revealed Truth

Even in the Church it was a long time before it came to be realized that the Bible is not intended to communicate scientific knowledge. We need only think of the case of Galileo, which indicates how difficult it is, even for us today, to rid oneself of certain preconceptions which are seemingly sanctioned and given the status of dogma by biblical revelation. There was, for instance, in the early part of this century, great disagreement concerning the way in which the biblical account of the creation (actually, there are two accounts) could be reconciled with the progress of scientific discovery of truth. Thus, in a sense, both the Bible and science became stumbling blocks, one to the other—on the one hand, the Bible seemed to deny the veracity of empirical deduction; and on the other hand, the truths of science seemed to deny the veracity of the word of God. In the attempt to find a compromise solution, a number of questionable theories were formulated: that the days of creation were really very long periods of time; or that, actually, the biblical account of creation was merely a "device" by which to impart other truths more pertinent to the time.

Only in recent years has theology, supported by some wise precepts of the magisterium, achieved a liberating breakthrough by which the Bible may now be seen in true perspective. We have come to understand the contemporary imagery and figurative language of the Bible's authors. God was able to "use" these men to make religious truths known, especially that truth which is decisive for man and his understanding of himself and the world—decisive, that is to say, for his life on earth and his salvation.

The historicity of revelation entails the fact that God enters into history in the views and languages of a particular time, and clothes in the thoughts of that time the ideas which he wishes to reveal. In our day, the Bible has been liberated, so to speak, from the gloss of historical circumstance, from its obligation to communicate human knowledge; so that now it is finally free to communicate to men the divine truths it contains.

Thus there is today general agreement that, so far from having any obligation of teaching natural science, the Bible on the contrary made use of its day's prevailing scientific concepts—or more accurately, of prevailing naïve mythological concepts—in order to make its religious revelational declarations in terms of those concepts. Henricus Renckens correctly says, "[The Israelite] possessed a whole body of profane knowledge about the past, according to his lights, and above all he had an explanation of it, which was based to a greater or lesser degree upon real events or known phenomena. Israel had no need to discover this body of contemporary 'science' for itself; it had imbibed it from its fellow peoples of the Mesopotamian basin as time went on. Thus when it became God's purpose to reveal himself to Israel, he found it already equipped, so to speak, with a whole world of ideas about all kinds of things, and in revealing the crucial saving events of the past to this people, he had to recken with a whole set of particular human ideas about the past which they already possessed. . . . God has grafted his revelation onto Israel's already existing human knowledge."*

Religious revelation is primarily concerned with those matters which affect man in his existence, which enable him to understand the meaning of his existence and the purpose of his earthly life. But because man is a part of creation, a being of the earth, and because his work is accomplished on the earth, and because he is subject to its conditions in his existence, it was inevitable that much was said to him in the Bible about the world. Even in order to understand himself, man is forced to make a "picture of the world" for himself; so that there are a number of basic questions about the world which, for his answers, man must have recourse to natural science. Was there a temporal beginning of the world, and will it at some time end? What is the significance of material, of the raw matter of this world, to which man in his bodily existence is also bound?

Now, it is not necessary for revelation to communicate

* *Israel's Concept of the Beginning*, New York, Herder and Herder, 1964, pp. 42–43.

some valid philosophical or scientific knowledge regarding these questions. But as for man's own self-understanding, revelation may not ignore questions as to how man should understand and judge his inclusion in the material world, and his superiority over all other earthly forms of life. In order for man to unlock the meaning of his existence, revelation must also tell him something about his own origin and that of the world, and about the purpose of all existence.

We can see, therefore, that there are a number of "border questions" between religion and science. Many such problems are still unresolved and under discussion, such as those regarding the course and the extent of world development; hominisation; poly- or monogenesis; the future of the world; eternal duration or an end of time; catastrophe or (merely) another beginning; a succession of changes or consummation. Even if modern science intentionally withdraws from debate on these questions, and skirts such problems in its research, man can never entirely ignore them, for his present self-understanding depends on answering them. In a like manner, anthropological questions stand at a point of intersection between science and religion: the relation of body and soul, all the aspects of man as seen in the oneness of his own self-knowledge, the differences of the sexes, differences in race and nationality, the unity of the human race, and so forth.

If these questions are to be discussed further, and they will have to be, it is important that the participants not expect the Bible to answer questions it is not qualified to answer. One must always look for the particularly religious meaning or connotation of a statement in the Bible, and in so doing, pay especial attention to the statement's literary genre.

Even so, however, revelation sets up certain "barriers" which prevent the researching scientist from drawing premature or possibly false conclusions from his limited store of knowledge. In fact, through revelation, the believing scientist can even establish certain guidelines for the formulation of his ideas about the world without having to deviate, in the course of his research, from strictly scientific method. The religious declaration of truth has a far more solid foundation than scientific research.

Revelation and the Science of History

Since revelation is closely related to history, in the sense that it actually takes place in history and is even concerned with certain definite facts and events of history, we will now attempt to delineate the more important and closer connections between the two.

The call of Abraham, father of the nation of Israel, took place in a historical moment, and the history of this people whom God chose to implement his plans for the salvation of men took place in a historical and geographical land which we know about through secular history. Due to the labors of archeologists, through the documents and monuments they have uncovered and brought to light, we can now verify many of the historical events and facts which are recorded in the historical books of the Old Testament. In many cases, it has been proved that "the Bible was right." But it would be a grave misunderstanding were we to turn to the Bible, in the matter of disputed questions, to learn the final answers to such questions of mortal, human history. The Bible does not consider history "as history." It is not at all concerned with "world history," in which, in any case, the small nation of Israel, dragged here and there by the powers of the Near East, played only a very minor role. In the midst of the historical events of the world, the Bible sees God at work—a God who possesses a very different measuring stick from that of men. God chose one of the smallest and least significant nations of the world to be his specially chosen people; he made Israel the people of God through whom he would effect his hidden plans for the world. "For you are a people holy to the Lord your God; the Lord your God has chosen you to be a people for his own possession, out of all the peoples that are on the face of the earth. It was not because you were more in number than any other people that the Lord set his love upon you and chose you, for you were the fewest of all peoples; but it is because the Lord loves you, and is keeping the oath which he swore to your fathers, that the Lord has brought you out with a mighty hand, and redeemed you from the house of bondage, from the hand of

23

Pharaoh king of Egypt" (Deut. 7, 6–8). The Bible deals with history only inasmuch as it is "salvation history"— which, however, is certainly no "superhistory" divorced from worldly events. It is, rather, worldly history insofar as it is meaningful for the salvation of men, insofar as God worked through it, and became recognizable through his workings by means of faith.

Even the greatest event of salvation, the sending of the Son of God, was accomplished in a moment of history. The sixfold date given in Lk. 3, 1f.—a synchronism so popular with the ancients—makes this fact especially evident. The ministry of Jesus of Nazareth was carried on in the public eye; and even the Roman historian Tacitus, who surely was more interested in things other than the execution of an apparently political revolutionist in the distant and un-settled land of Palestine, briefly reported to his readers the death of a certain religious zealot who had won many supporters—even as far as Rome itself. The history of Jesus Christ as such is not considered important in the New Testament. What is regarded as most significant is that the time finally came when God fulfilled his promises, and that he restored the Crucified One to life again, and "made him both Lord and Christ" (Acts 2, 36), "Author of life" (Acts 3, 15), in whom salvation was established and made possible for all men and for all time. Only if we have grasped this basic historical interpretation of the Bible as salvation history, in its unique historical vision, its special judgment on

24

history, and its idea of what is historically relevant, will we be able to judge its historical contents fairly.

Moreover, the New Testament did not record and relate the historical events of its time according to the strict standards of our present-day science of history, but rather, like the rest of the ancient world, was under the influence of and subserved the world-views, the modes of literary expression, and the mores of the day. If one is not aware of this fact, one can easily envision a false "historicity" in the Bible, and too readily define various historical statements in the Bible as "heresies," contradictions, or inaccuracies. The biblical writers related the course of events of their time in a very free and easy manner, and were often unconcerned with exact circumstance. They did not intend to provide "documentaries," protocol, or reportage. What was most important to them was not the foreground occurrences, but rather the deeper divine meaning of the history of salvation "hid" behind the outward experiences and worldy events, which could be seen and understood only by the eyes of the believer.

Matters remained in a somewhat unhealthy state for a long time, until biblical science freed itself from narrow-minded apologetics, and came to recognize and honor the Bible in a positive way. Now it knows that it is necessary to take into account the literary genre of biblical narrative, inquire into the personal approach and intentions of the author, study the views and opinions of earlier times and other civilizations; above all, biblical science has learned that it is neces-

25

sary to pay strict attention to the particular religious lesson or thought which it was the narrative's first purpose to convey. This progress in the scientific treatment of scriptural narratives and statements was observed and encouraged in the biblical encyclicals of the popes from Leo XIII to Pius XII.

Progress in biblical science does not mean, however, that it has renounced the historical value of the books of the Bible. All that has happened is that biblical science has become "free" to see the statements and allusions of the Bible in correct historical perspective, and thereby penetrate straight to the real, what we might call the raw contents of revelation. This kind of perception is especially important when biblical exegesis examines such controverted questions as the "historical Jesus" and whether he is or is not the "Christ of faith."

The Religious Assertion of Truth in the Bible

Thus we have removed a few stumbling blocks and cleared the way for an understanding of the Bible in light of its proper function as the word of God. If we examine the Bible in the correct manner, that is, if we take into account its unique point of view, and make our judgments accordingly, then truly we can come to hear its word as the word of God and learn to understand its profound message. The express purpose of the Bible in all its books is a religious one, namely, to reveal to men the thoughts of God about men, so that men can find him and work out their salvation. These revelations of God's thoughts are not always readily accessible, not always "on the surface," its accessibility depending, so to speak, on the ratio between the word of God and man's word, and on the degree of historical limitation "imposed" on revelation. Very often, therefore, it is not at all easy to determine the actual revelation-content of a particular passage written in any of the innumerable literary styles of the Bible.

But now let us pose a twofold question: Does God really want to give us a concrete, understandable presentation of revelation, formulated in clear and well-defined phrases; or does he not, rather, simply want to summon us with his revelation, to confront us personally, to place us in a position of decision as we work out our salvation before him? This is an important question, for there is a new trend in theology today, the existential interpretation of the Bible, which is *not* first of all concerned to know what the Bible says about God, man, the world, history. These existential theologians have discovered a very important aspect of revelation, they have brought to light what we have for a long time generally overlooked or not given sufficient attention to. However, in denying any revealed content, they have gone to the extreme of diminishing, disfiguring, or even voiding biblical revelation. There are certain "doctrines" and "truths" which

27

revelation communicates. We should never regard these truths and doctrines as something isolated and detached from the revealing God, for there is only one divine truth which is the divine revelation.

An example of such "existential" interpretation of revelation is found in the theology of Rudolf Bultmann. In an essay titled "The Concept of Revelation in the New Testament" in his book, *Existence and Faith,** Bultmann sets up as his basic axiom that the subject and object of revelation is not a series of propositions or body of dogma, but that it is neither more nor less than the living God himself. He rejects the view, therefore, that revelation consists in "the communication of knowledge or of doctrine." He continues: "What, then, has been revealed? Nothing at all, so far as the question concerning revelation asks for doctrines—doctrines, say, that no man could have discovered for himself—or for mysteries that become known once and for all as soon as they are communicated. On the other hand, however, everything has been revealed, insofar as man's eyes are opened concerning his own existence and he is once again able to understand himself."†

While Bultmann is correct in stressing the existential aspect of revelation, he is wrong in overstressing it to the point where revelation is seen in an entirely relative and subjective way. God's selection of Israel as his chosen people,

* London, Hodder & Stoughton, 1961.
† Pages 66, 85–86.

his historical relations with that people, the appearances and messages of the prophets, the demands of Jesus, the gathering of the apostles and giving them a mission, the establishment of the Church, the salvific role of the Church and her awareness of this role, the requirement of baptism for membership in the Church, would be completely meaningless if God wanted to call each man personally, and give him, in exclusion of all other things but himself, a new understanding of his own existence.

The historically revealing God shows man—all men—an historical, concrete way to attain salvation. Certainly, man must make decisions for himself, but not only and merely about what he has discovered in himself, or about his potential as a human being, but also and especially about God's own precepts and directives. Man, placed in a position where he is alone and confronted with the ultimate questions of his existence, finds that he is in darkness; and revelation is the light which God, from outside this darkness, gives to him in revelation so that he can make his way. Revelation communicates truths to man which he could never know with sufficient clarity by his own resources; and besides, revelation is not given to him merely for his intellectual satisfaction, but that he may find his goal in life, and the way to attain that goal.

In many parts of the Bible the religious assertion of truth is immediately evident. Thus in the Old Testament God showed his union with, spiritual ties to, and superiority over the Israelite people that was surrounded by a heathen world which worshiped false gods. He revealed his holy will, his law which, in the form of covenant, obliged the Israelites to be faithful to the cult of Yahweh. Through the prophets he promised a time of future salvation and peace for Israel and all the nations; he promised the fulfillment of man's deepest desire for deliverance and salvation.

In the New Testament, Jesus speaks of the coming of the reign of God, of man's need to worship God totally and exclusively, of the great commandment of love of God and neighbor. Jesus' message was one of unprecedented radicalness, and it cannot be understood differently.

But now let us treat of those questions which stem from the close connection between the divine word of God and the word of men in time. For example, how are we to understand those statements of Jesus concerning the future which are clothed in apocalyptical language? What about the proximate announcement—or rather the proximate expectation—of the Parousia, of the world to come? As to the apostolic teachings in the epistles—for example, concerning the behavior vis-à-vis the state, the question of slavery, the organization and condition of the community—to what extent are these teachings conditioned by time and history? There is far more still to be considered. But we must never forget that the primary purpose of the Bible is not the enlightenment of human problems, not a directive in human business, but religious revelation.

3. THE SALVIFIC CHARACTER OF REVEALED TRUTH

In order better to understand the religious orientation of the Bible, we must be clear on yet another peculiarity of revelation, namely, that revelation is always accomplished from the point of view of man's salvation. No matter that in the final analysis it serves unto the glorification of God: it is still wrong to presume that God ever wished merely to afford us a deeper insight into his essence and into his world. Whatever he reveals of himself and of his thought always aims at joining man yet closer to himself, leading him nearer to himself and so directing him along the way of life. The most famous manifestation of God in the Old Testament—to Moses, in the burning bush (Ex. 3)—is not meant to disclose the metaphysical essence of God, but rather to reveal the constant and faithful "God of the fathers." The explanation of his name Yahweh as "He Who Is"—the Greek Bible translates this with "the Being One"—does not serve as a speculation as to the being and nature of God, but rather to bind the Israelites in trust to him who spoke to their fathers Abraham, Isaac, and Jacob—who is, in effect, *their God*. And now this God has decided to liberate them from misery, from slavery in Egypt, and to lead them into the land promised to their fathers. Again, the event on Sinai was more than the manifestation of the greatness and grandeur of God: it was rather a revelation decisive for the

31

life and future of the people of Israel. "You have seen what I did to the Egyptians, and how I bore you on eagles' wings and brought you to myself. Now therefore, if you will obey my voice and keep my covenant, you shall be my own possession among all peoples; for all the earth is mine, and you shall be to me a kingdom of priests and a holy nation" (Ex. 19, 4ff.). The commitment to law will bind Israel to Yahweh, who is "merciful and gracious, slow to anger and abounding in steadfast love and faithfulness . . . forgiving iniquity and transgression and sin, but who will by no means clear the guilty, visiting the iniquity of the fathers upon the children and the children's children" (Ex. 34, 6f.). The Torah, the divine law, was therefore thought of not as a burden, but as a mark of distinction for Israel, and the people of God were well aware of their grave responsibility, as is emphasized in Deut. 30, 11ff.: "For this commandment which I command you this day is not too hard for you, neither is it far off. . . . But the word is very near you; it is in your mouth and in your heart, so that you can do it. See, I have set before you this day life and good, death and evil." The man who submits to the will and the law of God experiences already in this life the joy and blessing of communion with God, as the psalmists so often confess. The man who rejoices in the law of God is like a tree growing at the edge of a brook, which brings forth its fruit in due time (see Ps. 1, 2f.). And so the pious man says to God: "Thou dost show me the path of life; in thy presence there is fullness of joy, in thy right hand are pleasures for evermore" (Ps. 16, 11); ". . . with thee is the fountain of life; in thy light do we see light" (36, 9).

It is because of the salvific nature of revelation that the Bible does not reveal everything to man, does not reveal everything at once, does not reveal everything in utter clarity. In any given situation, God reveals only as much as is necessary or useful for the salvation of man in his particular situation: we might call this the *economy of revelation*. There are many examples of this economy in the Old Testament, and in fact the entire New Testament is always open to further revelation. There is here a constant progression from promise to fulfillment, and from that fulfillment to a new promise. There is a steady progression into an ever open future, so that the full and entire revelation can be expected only in the final fulfillment of the eschatological future.

We may find an example of the historical limitation or restriction of Old Testament revelation in the awareness that salvation then was thought of in terms of property and prosperity, fertility and longevity. Such an orientation would point to the earthbound, materialistic over-all attitude which characterized Israel at that time. And yet that nation was well aware of its utter dependence on Yahweh, and would not be entirely overwhelmed by worldly considerations. The notion of an afterlife in the presence and fellowship of God, and the certainty of a future resurrection, developed much

33

later. The same is true of the expectation of a definitive time
of salvation. There was great uncertainty concerning the
person of the promised redeemer, the anointed king of the
Parousia, the Messiah; it was even less clear how one was
to recognize with certainty his appearance and his activity.
Therefore, the true Messiah, Jesus of Nazareth, was for his
contemporaries an enigma, a stumbling block, come "for
the fall and rising of many in Israel, and for a sign that is
spoken against" (Lk. 2, 34). Here again, revelation coerces
to decision, releasing no man from the obligation to respond
in faith. Even through the prophets, God spoke with some
obscurity. His threats and warnings are comprehensible
enough, as are his promises for the future; but as the God
of salvation he remains hidden: we must believe—we must
make our commitment to him. This is the divine pedagogy
in the economy of revelation.

Biblical revelation culminates in the message and teaching
of Jesus Christ, the Son of God. At this point, its salvific
character is disclosed in perfect clarity, for this last ambassador from God proclaims nothing other than the boundless
mercy of God towards fallen humanity. To save these lost
ones is the joy of God, a satisfaction beyond human comprehension—as is illustrated in Lk. 15, that "Gospel within the
Gospel." No one realized or understood more perfectly than
did St. John this desire of God aimed only at the salvation
of man in the sending of his Son. "For God sent the Son
into the world, not to condemn the world, but that the world

might be saved through him" (Jn. 3, 17). The revelation of
the Son has no other purpose; and yet John is also aware of
the critical function of this eschatological revelation of the
Son—broadly speaking, of the word of God to mankind.
"He who believes in him is not condemned; he who does
not believe is condemned already, because he has not believed in the name of the only Son of God" (Jn. 3, 18).

For this reason, even the revelation of the Son does not
lift all obscurity for human vision and understanding. Even
now, we walk ". . . by faith, not by sight" (2 Cor. 5, 7). This
is particularly true of our road into the future: our own
individual road and that of all mankind. A heavy veil yet
obscures the end of the present world and the dawn of the
new and perfected creation. Jesus refrained from answering
all apocalyptical questions pertaining to the time of Parousia,
what this end would be like, the number of the elect, the
conditions of the world to come; these he left to the
sovereignty of God. It is enough for us that God in his might
will one day give us the fullness of salvation and the glory
of his kingdom. It is enough for us to know in faith that we
are now children of God—even though it is not yet clear
what we will one day become (1 Jn. 3, 2). It is enough for
us to know that the Son of God came unto us and gave us
insight to know him who is true (1 Jn. 5, 20f.). This is the
knowledge of salvation necessary to us; for he who knows
the Son, he also has life.

So now we may better understand the introductory phrase

of this chapter: ". . . and the truth will make you free." It is the truth of the divine revelation of life brought by the Son, as we read a little further on: ". . . if the Son makes you free, you will be free indeed" (Jn. 8, 36). The phrase is not a general statement regarding the uplifting and liberating quality of all manner of truth, but a most clear and unambiguous statement about the truth of revelation, present to us in the Son of God, which will lead us—provided we accept it in faith—to that true, ultimate human freedom which is life with God.

II.

God's Truth in Human Dress

"In many and various ways God spoke of old to our fathers by the prophets; but in these last days he has spoken to us by a Son, . . ." (Heb. 1, 1f.).

In this magnificent introduction to the Letter to the Hebrews, the author expresses the opinion that "the Son," Jesus Christ, has brought to men the last, complete, and absolute revelation of God. At the same time, he has witnessed to the authenticity of revelation, for "In many and various ways" God had already spoken to men. His revelation had begun hundreds of years before, when he made known his thoughts and plans to the fathers of the old covenant. It was a true and valid revelation. Then he chose for himself a number of select spokesmen, the "prophets," and these men from time to time addressed their contemporaries, they revealed God's holy will to them and pointed out the path of salvation. The language and modes of expression changed, but God's word, the communication of the unchanging, eternal, holy God to mankind, in its own historical situations, did not cease. The Bible is the witness of

37

God speaking to man down through the ages; it is a many-kinded witness, choired by many spokesmen. God's word reaches us in nothing other than in our own human language.

However, because divine revelation comes to men "dressed" in their own language, a number of questions arise concerning the "truth" of revelation: for how can God adequately express his thoughts in human language; and to what extent is it possible for human words and concepts to express the spirit contained within the thought? How certain can we be in determining what is God's word and what man's word in the Bible? Is such a distinction ultimately impossible? To what extent is the word of God binding on the actual historical situation when it was revealed, and to what extent on future generations? Can future generations understand an historical revelation in the same way as former generations? Especially must we ask questions about the eschatological revelation of Jesus, for it was first intended for a special moment in history, namely, for the time of the earthly ministry of the Messiah. These historical difficulties seem, indeed, to jeopardize the absoluteness of revealed truth.

Even the Fathers of the Church reflected on the way in which the word of God has come to us in human language. Origen, the greatest biblical scholar of ancient times, compared the transformation of divine revelation into human language with the incarnation of the *Logos*. "By becoming body and flesh," Origen wrote, "the divine *Logos* has achieved the ability of proclaiming himself to men in word and writing . . . The Bible is God's perfect and harmonious means of expression" ("Mt.," fr. 11). "The entire Scripture is the single, perfect body of the Word" ("Jer.-Hom.," fr. 2). In his commentary on Jn. 1, 27 (". . . even he who comes after me, the thong of whose sandal I am not worthy to untie"), Origen says, " 'The thong of the sandal' gives us to understand the word of God in this way, that it effects what it plans for mankind not by assuming the form of divinity, but rather by 'taking the role of a servant,' so that the way of the actualization of salvation is obscured" (fr. 18). The transformation of God's word into human language, therefore, is a "kenosis," that is, an emptying, similar to the kenosis of the divine *Logos* in the incarnation.

In a more allegorical interpretation, Origen explains Jesus' washing of the feet of the apostles thus: "Putting away [emptying himself of] all finery . . . Jesus becomes bare in his 'servant's role.' Not merely in order to be bare, but rather to be able to dry the feet of his disciples with a suitable cloth after he has washed them, '. . . he took a linen and girded himself with it.' The meaning of this is: Consider how the great and splendid Word diminished himself in becoming flesh in order to wash the feet of the apostles. 'He poured water into the basin,' relates the evangelist. But the water, as I see it, is the Word which washes the feet of the apostles when they come to the basin held by Jesus" ("On Jn.," 32,

39

4). This is a profound and instructive view of the insoluble union between God's word and the word of man.

St. John Chrysostom, who has left us so many rich commentaries, thinks no differently. He speaks often of the condescension (συγκατάβασις, *condescendentia*) of God to man in the word of the Bible. God has "descended" to us that we might attain him through human words, and thus be able to understand his profound message. And the greatest of the Latin Church Fathers, St. Augustine, once wrote very briefly and precisely: "God has spoken to man in a human way" (*The City of God,* bk. 17, ch. 6, 2), and St. Thomas Aquinas elaborated on this idea ("On Heb. 1," lect. 4). Even the fact of inspiration does not stand in the way of this interpretation, but indeed acknowledges it. God is the first and foremost originator (*auctor primarius*) of holy Scripture, but man also is the actual author. God uses man as his medium, as the instrument of revelation; but, corresponding to his own nature as a being endowed with reason, the human writer as instrument is moved by his own thoughts and opinions, and yet "reproduces" God's revelation.

The relation of divine inspiration and human coöperation is indeed difficult to define. By reason of its divine authorship, the Scriptures are "inerrant," but this allegation can easily be misunderstood. The biblical statements are "true" in that they say what the human author intended to say. This means, however, that we must pay attention to the particular purpose of the author when he wrote what he did, as well as to the literary form which he used in writing.

But let us now turn to the word of Scripture itself. How did the revealed truth become molded in human language? How did this kenosis of God's word in holy Scripture happen?

1. REVELATION CIRCUMSCRIBED BY HUMAN LANGUAGE

The fact that God employed language and words for communicating his revelation is not something which is self-evident in itself, but which even so serves as revelation's "trademark." In a number of nonchristian religions, another kind of "revelation" was and very often still is taught. It is the "revelation" that man becomes a partaker of through rapturous ecstasy, or a transcendental vision, or a mystical interior experience of the divine.

There are signs of such thinking in the environment of early Christianity, especially in Hellenistic mysticism—for example, in the hermetical writings. However, Christianity remained critically opposed to this kind of "revelation," as did the Jewish religion. Even when in the Bible it is reported that the prophets had visions, it is a matter of secondary importance. Alone and decisive in real importance is the revelation of the word, the "utterance of Yahweh," which the prophets as God's spokesmen made known to men. God revealed himself in the medium of words, and

41

indeed, in human words of a human language in a human time.

In order to understand how the word of God was transplanted into human language, we must study a few examples from Scripture. At the same time, we can observe not only how far the word of God descended to mankind at a particular time, but also, as the case often was, how human language was ennobled by being the means of God's communication of revelation.

The Accommodation of Divine Revelation in Human Language

As a first example of the language of revelation we can take the vision of Isaiah at the time of his calling. The prophet sees ". . . the Lord sitting upon a throne, high and lifted up; and his train filled the temple. Above him stood two seraphim" singing the praise of the thrice-holy Lord of hosts. "And the foundations of the thresholds shook at the voice of him who called, and the house was filled with smoke." And one of the seraphim takes a burning coal from the altar and with it touches the lips of the prophet (Is. 6, 1–7). We can see how the heavenly throne room of God is described just like the sanctuary of Yahweh on earth, the temple of Jerusalem. And yet it is not really described; rather something is hinted at in images which obscure more than they disclose. For the focal point of this vision of the calling is the choosing, the ordination, the sending of Isaiah in the office of prophet into the midst of a rebellious people. The glowing coal from the heavenly altar cleanses his lips of all iniquity, and now he must proclaim with purified lips the message of God. It is a hard and troublesome message, a message of judgment, of the devastation of the land, of the desolation of cities. Only at the very end there lies a consoling promise, the promise of a remnant, a holy seed.

This is a very human, a more "stuttering" than illuminating story, and yet imbedded in it is a very profound divine idea: that the many have been stubborn and that a holy remnant has been chosen, that a rule and a law, a covenant, will determine salvation history from now on.

If we turn to the only prophetical book of the New Testament, the Revelation of St. John, we see that the case is very much the same: here is a very picturesque language using many images and symbols, many of which are difficult for us today to understand because of the book's apocalyptical style and historical allusions; but in essence, it is a very clear, inclusive prophecy which only says what Jesus himself revealed to us about the time before the end of the world, about the Parousia, the resurrection and the judgment, and the final kingdom of God.

There is a second example of a messianic prophecy in the Old Testament. Balaam, the divinely inspired seer, was taken to the steppes of Moab, where he was to call down a blessing instead of a curse on the sons of Israel. His words accord with the mentality of the time, and are spoken in a particular historical situation. Later, however, they are seen to have been a secret oracle about the future. Balaam cries out, "I see him, but not now; I behold him, but not nigh: a star shall come forth out of Jacob, and a scepter shall rise out of Israel; it shall crush the forehead of Moab, and break down all the sons of Sheth" (Num. 24, 17). Who is this ruler from Israel? Is it Saul, who warred with the Moabites, or David, who overcame them, and put many of them to death?

There is more to the picture, however. At the time of the reign of David, the prophet Nathan prophesied to the King, "And your house and your kingdom shall be made sure for ever before me; your throne shall be established for ever" (2 Sam. 7, 16). But David's dynasty perished. But then another oracle prophesied in the Book of Amos: "In that day I will raise up the booth of David that is fallen and repair its breaches, and raise up its ruins, and rebuild it as in the days of old; that they may possess the remnant of Edom and all the nations who are called by my name . . ." (9, 11–12).

Israel at the time of Jesus longed for that Son of David, the Messiah, the redeemer and reconstructor of the nation. But the fulfillment came to pass in another manner: the Messiah, poor and humble, entered the holy city seated upon an ass, according to the prophecy of Zechariah—not as a war hero, but as the prince of peace. Only the disciples of Jesus

—and they only after Easter—understood the ancient word of revelation, and Peter announced it on Pentecost: "Let all the house of Israel therefore know assuredly that God has made him both Lord and Christ, this Jesus whom you crucified" (Acts 2, 36). At the Council of the Apostles, St. James refers specifically to the prophecy of Amos concerning the "booth of David that is fallen," and now understands the fulfillment of the words that *all nations* seek the Lord. Even the heathens draw near and join the people of God.

In a similar manner, we might examine many another prophecy of ancient days, oracles which are dark and mysterious until they become comprehensible in the light of fulfillment. God's revelation remains throughout the centuries until it finds ultimate formulation in the eschatological revelation of his Son. And yet, not even the Son's revelation can show us everything in perfect clarity. Instead, much remains prophecy and mystery until in the perfection of salvation in the world to come, even these veils shall be lifted.

There is a third example: the revelation concerning the beginning and the end of the world—about creation and completion. How much has been written concerning the account of creation in Genesis; how much has it been disputed and ridiculed! We are all aware that this is a naïve and ingenuous, and yet wonderfully poetic, representation of an earlier picture of the world which we have long ago rolled up and tucked away into a corner. The question is, however, whether it is anything more than a myth, just as it is told in similar form by many nonchristian peoples.

Fortunately, however, Christians are no longer under the illusion that the Bible can give them a scientific explanation of the origin and development of the universe; and so we have become free and ripe to hear the revealing word of God. The naïve language of the Bible discloses religious truths which are independent of the progress of scientific research: that the world came into existence out of nothing solely through the will of God; that man is called to be lord over all the earth, but at the same time servant of God; that through a grave fault man was dispelled from the divine order and lost peace with God; —but it is unnecessary to elaborate further.

The same is true concerning the revelation of the last things. What New Testament revelation presents to us is nothing other than a great religious interpretation of the history of the world and of mankind. This interpretation, as revelation, is accepted by the faithful. But for the non-believer, the question remains, whether it is possible to find a better answer as to the meaning of existence and the enigmatic course of history.

God's revelation in human language is plain and simple, yet impenetrably profound. We see this in the New Testament, in the language of Jesus. Even the Son, who brings us a direct message from God, speaks no other language save that of his own time. He makes use of simple images and parables, of examples from daily life; he speaks so that the common people can understand. And yet what tremendous power there is often in his words: "But I say to you, Do not swear at all, either by heaven, for it is the throne of God, or by the earth, for it is his footstool, or by Jerusalem, for it is the city of the great King" (Mt. 5, 34f.).

We mark the reserve of Jesus whenever he speaks of heavenly things. In telling of the coming of the kingdom he avoids ornamental language, but rather uses familiar imagery, such as the meal or the harvest, or introduces new images, such as the pearl of great price or the leavened dough. God can only be spoken of in analogies, represented by human symbols such as lord, king, father of a household. His boundless mercy and goodness can be expressed only by comparison with the behavior of men: "Or what man of you, if his son asks him for bread, will give him a stone? Or if he asks for a fish will give him a serpent? If you then, who are evil, know how to give good gifts to your children, how much more will your Father who is in heaven give good things to those who ask him!" (Mt. 7, 9ff.). The infinite mercy of God so far surpasses human comprehension that it can be described only in paradoxical parables: a father who not only forgives his son fallen to the depth of shame and wickedness, but even orders a great celebration in his honor and restores him to his filial right; a king who commends the steward who has been squandering the royal wealth; a man who pays a full day's wages to men who have worked but one hour; a householder who himself waits on his vigilant and faithful servants. We need only read the Gospel to be impressed again by the vital, moving language of Jesus. God in his revelation has surely become closely united with men through their language—often their daily language.

The Adaptation of Human Language
to Divine Revelation

Occasionally, the divine condescension elevated—sublimated —the human language. Even outside of Christianity, religious language often developed a special "holy style." In his famous work *Agnostos Theos. Studies in the History of Form of Religious Language,** E. Norden assembled much material on the subject. The language of revelation also has a particular style, as Rudolf Bultmann and his followers have shown, particularly of the Gnostic literature. Why should we not admit the formative influence of environment on the literary genre and style of biblical revelation? If God made use of men, entering into their word with his own, he would surely allow for the influence of time and environment on the language of the mediators of revelation, since the differentiation of meaning is effected not in form but in content. But because content and form are mutually de-

* Stuttgart, 1956.

pendent, the linguistic "dress" of biblical revelation is quite marked; and this must not be forgotten in the study of religious history. This again is an example of the way in which the thought and consciousness of divine revelation often shaped and ennobled the language of the Bible.

We turn to the Book of Deuteronomy for an example of the way in which human language is sublimated by its use as a medium of revelation. This book is a new rendering of the divine revelation to Moses on Mount Sinai, in the form of a speech given by that patriarch to his people before his death, before the entry of the Israelites into Canaan. The language of this "second giving of the law" is wonderfully refined as befits its lofty subject. We need only recall those passages which form the major part of the Jewish *shema* recited twice daily: "Hear, O Israel: The Lord our God is one Lord; and you shall love the Lord your God with all your heart, and with all your soul, and with all your might. And these words which I command you this day shall be upon your heart..." (6, 4–6; see also 6, 7–9; 11, 13–21). The same thought pervades the entire book: "Keep silence and hear, O Israel: this day you have become the people of the Lord your God. You shall therefore obey the voice of the Lord your God, keeping his commandments and his statutes, which I command you this day" (27, 9f.). Does this language not express most perfectly the essence of the Old Testament religion? The thought of election and obligation; the awareness of having received God's revelation and law, and of the simultaneous duty of obedience and fidelity; the knowledge of God's blessing and his curse on the people of the covenant —all these find expression in this language. We can also see in the prophetic language the august style of the divine self-assertion ("I, Yahweh," etc.).

In the New Testament we find the same majestic turns of phrase on the lips of Jesus. He adopts the phrase "I am" in the Gospel of St. John. "I am the light of the world; he who follows me will not walk in darkness, but will have the light of life" (8, 12); "... I am the way, the truth, and the life ..." (14, 6); "... before Abraham was, I am" (8, 58).

Christ's language as recorded by the synoptic writers is also marked by those stylistic peculiarities which underline its revelational character.

Heinz Schürmann has gathered such observations and classified them, remarking: "In the words of the Lord recorded in Scripture, we find certain idiosyncrasies which betray the exalted self-confidence of the speaker. The language of the Christ sounds alien, unfamiliar, solemn, sublime, significant, remarkable: it has a very particular eschatological actuality. Most important, it is powerfully decisive and authoritative."*

A most impressive scene is the last one in the Gospel of St. Matthew, where the risen *Kyrios,* having newly reassumed power, sends the disciples forth into the world: "All

---

* "The Language of the Christ," in *Biblische Zeitschrift,* 1958, pp. 54–84; this excerpt from p. 55.

authority in heaven and on earth has been given to me. Go therefore and make disciples of all nations. . . ; and lo, I am with you always, to the close of the age" (28, 18ff.).

In the heavenly hymns of praise of the Book of Revelation we find yet another example of the way in which revelation forms the language, how the revelation of Christ produces an unmistakable Christian style which is intensified to the point of cultic solemnity. These hymns are formed out of the words of revelation and ring down consolingly and encouragingly from the heavens. They are triumphal chants taken up on earth by the martyr-Church tried with affliction. The song at the opening of the seven-sealed scroll is in praise of the Lamb: "Worthy art thou to take the scroll and to open its seals, for thou wast slain and by thy blood didst ransom men for God from every tribe and tongue and people and nation, and hast made them a kingdom and priests to our God, and they shall reign on earth" (5, 9f.).

At the destruction of the great whore Babylon, the symbol of the godless and evil power of the world, the seer perceives ". . . what seemed to be the voice of a great multitude, like the sound of many waters and like the sound of many thunderpeals, crying, 'Hallelujah! For the Lord our God the Almighty reigns. Let us rejoice and give him glory, for the marriage of the Lamb has come, and his Bride has made herself ready . . ." (19, 6f.). As faith responds to the divine revelation, the human language, in the repetition and transmission of the message, in the proclamation and in the cult, is raised to a style befitting the occasion, so to speak: that is, as being words of revelation.

2. REVELATION BOUND TO HUMAN HISTORY

The historicity of revelation is evident already in the fact of its embodiment in human language. For God's revelation was issued to men of historical existence, men of a definite time and environment, through whom revelation was mediated and transmitted. But the ingrafting of revelation in human history is of even more profound significance; the condescension of God to men becomes even more conspicuous therein. God has intervened in human history; revelation having come down through these many centuries has fashioned a distinct revelation history.

Revelation History Before the Definitive Revelation of Jesus Christ

It was many centuries before the appearance on earth of God's eschatological revealer—his own Son. We will again take a number of examples to illustrate the significance of this fact.

We know that even Israel had no clear conception of life after death. Certainly, there was the idea of life continued in the realm of the dead (*sheol*), but this was no more than a shadowy existence, a kind of shabby earthly existence lacking the freshness and vigor of this life—it was a dark and melancholy life that was envisioned there. This is a view taken from the earliest revelation, but it played an important role in the history of divine revelation; for God wished to divulge to his people above all those fundamental truths which they were to know and heed, surrounded as they were by heathen folk, in order to become his own people and to perform his priestly office in the world. For this to be effected, God's uniqueness and spirituality were necessary: his creation and rule of the world; his election of Israel to be the people of the covenant; his mighty saving and protecting leadership; his holy law and obligatory cult. It was this consciousness which distinguished Israel, for the belief in the dead and the invocation of spirits were prevalent also in the surrounding nations.

On the other hand, the very mysteriousness of death could awaken strong religious feeling, as evidenced by the Psalms. Only after the Exile, with the strengthening of the eschatological expectation, did the belief in life after death, in a future resurrection, assume a tangible form. In the times of greatest humiliation, during the battles of the days of the Maccabees, the belief in resurrection was both a motivation and a consolation. Thus we hear the Maccabean martyrs cry out in the midst of their torment: "Thou indeed, O most wicked man, destroyest us out of this present life: but the King of the world will raise us up, who die for his laws, in the resurrection of eternal life" (2 Mac. 7, 9); "It is better, being put to death by men, to look for hope from God, to be raised up again by him: for, as to thee, thou shalt have no resurrection unto life" (7, 14). It is certain that the Greek belief in immortality had its influence (see the Book of Wisdom) in the last two centuries before Christ. God's revelation built on this belief.

All of this shows how deeply divine revelation is ingrained into human history. At the same time, we must not think of the belief in the resurrection as having developed as a matter of course out of the temper of the time. At the time of Jesus, the belief in the resurrection of the body was by no means universally accepted. The Sadducees, for example, rejected this belief. To their questions in this regard, Jesus gave the authoritative reply: "Is not this why you are wrong, that you know neither the scriptures nor the power of God?" And then, having given his own interpretation of certain parts of the Old Testament: ". . . you are quite wrong" (Mk. 12, 18–27 and parallels). In matters of faith, therefore, the final instance remains the word of God as authoritatively interpreted by Jesus.

A second example of the economy of divine revelation may be found in the messianic prophecies already referred to above. The prophets speaking to their contemporaries of the redeemer who was to come could not specify the exact time of his appearance nor the details of his life and work. Their foretelling was meant to enkindle hope in the hearts of the people, so that they might walk through times of darkness with confidence into the future. The ancient prophecies became comprehensible only in the light of fulfillment. Only with the advent of Jesus did it become clear who was *Emmanuel* ("God with us") foretold by Isaiah (7, 14ff.). Therefore, the early Church could see many of the prophecies fulfilled in Jesus; for example, that of the suffering "servant of God" of Is. 53, or that of the "Son of man" who, according to Dan. 7, 13, was to appear on the clouds of heaven. Jesus was indeed the "Son of man"; but at the same time, the prophecies of Daniel and Jesus' own words strengthened the hope in his second coming. Here we see that even the eschatological revelation of Jesus leaves open a number of expectations for the future. We must observe this last Word of God in its historical and salvation-historical perspective.

The Eschatological Revelation of Jesus and Its Historical Ties

Even the revelation mission of Jesus remains under the law of the economy of salvation and revelation. The last ambassador from God took up the religious thought and the expectation of salvation of his time, and in that decisive hour proclaimed the appearance of the new divine message of salvation, God's offer of grace, the Gospel. But even the most faithful of the disciples could not comprehend the total plan of God, and least of all that way of suffering and death which God had determined for his Messiah. Only by little could Jesus initiate even them into that great mystery (see Mk. 8, 31ff. and parallels). Not until the resurrection of Jesus—and under the guidance of the Paraclete—was the great salvation event made clear to the apostles and the early Church.

The fourth evangelist grasped this economy of revelation profoundly. He has Jesus say to his disciples at the last supper: "I have many things to say to you, but you cannot bear them now. When the Spirit of truth comes, he will guide you into all the truth; ..." (16, 12f.). Even in the New Testament, then, there remain such things as must be disclosed and emphasized in the revelation of Jesus: this task was entrusted to the apostles.

We shall now take some examples of the way in which this expansion of revelation took place already within the New Testament.

After the resurrection, the Christology contained in the yet obscure self-assertion of Jesus began slowly to develop. At first the focal point was the way of Jesus through humiliation on the cross to elevation unto God. That is, he who had once come in lowliness was awaited in his exaltation in the Parousia. The titles and names of honor bestowed upon him increased in number and kind. Above all, he was acclaimed as the *Kyrios,* the Lord enthroned at the right hand of God, who had overcome the ungodly powers and was receiving cultic praise from his congregation. This placing of Jesus at the side of God only served to emphasize his own divinity, as Old Testament references to God as *Kyrios* were transferred to Christ (see Rom. 10, 13; Phil. 2, 10f.). It followed that the heavenly preëxistence of the Son of God was emphasized, as witness the passage Phil. 2, 6–11. The Letter to the Colossians points up the cosmic significance of Christ, his mediation in creation and redemption (Col. 1, 15–20). Similarly, the Letter to the Ephesians pays tribute to his sovereignty over the Church and indeed over the entire cosmos. Other interpretations of the uniqueness of the person of Christ appear in the Johannine *Logos*-Christology, and in the statements concerning "the Son" of the Letter to the Hebrews.

It is vital to avoid misunderstanding this Christological development as though the man Jesus gradually was transformed into the manlike Son of God, or as though there had evolved a myth of a divine being which descended from heaven, became man, and redeemed all men. Rather is the following true: these categories, these declarations about the nature of Jesus grew out of Jesus' own revelation of himself, and out of the faith of the early Church in her interpretation of that revelation corresponding to her own powers of recognition and expression, whether it be Palestinian or Hellenic Judaeo-Christianity, or pagan Christianity, influenced somewhat by numerous spiritual currents. These developments took place quite speedily, coming to completion still in apostolic times, so that the aspostolic authority is noticeable in all the New Testament documents, even those which do not proceed directly from the apostles.

Similar remarks may be made with regard to ecclesiology, the Church's understanding of herself, the penetration of her theologians. Old Testament ideas, particularly that of the "people of God," were taken up, as were various corresponding images—the holy temple, the holy city, the planting, the flock of God. All of this is consistent with the fact that Jesus wanted to gather the eschatological community of God, and to bring to completion God's plan for Israel. But the unbelief in Israel at the time of Jesus created a new and different situation, so that the people of God were therefore placed in quite different circumstances by the propitiatory death of Jesus. The effusion of the Holy Spirit soon brought the community of Christ to the consciousness of its eschatological existence; and at the same time, the Letter to the Hebrews demonstrated the wandering people of God as still aiming at the heavenly goal. The historical existence and progress of the Church, especially in regard to her mission, inspired new ideas and opened up new perspectives. The pagan contingent which entered the Church indeed left its external mark, but at the same time permitted the rise of a Church as a Judaeo-pagan amalgam (see Eph.). We see in this context a growth of recognition and awareness of what Jesus did and said, intended and set forth, regarding his Church and her mission.

It would be instructive, finally, to observe the early

Church's view of the Holy Spirit, who was at first considered simply as the great eschatological gift of God. St. Paul saw him more clearly as the Spirit of the risen Lord, as his Life streaming over the faithful, as the "first installment" towards salvation, and as a surety of future resurrection for all united to Christ. St. John gives him more personal characteristics, as aide and advocate, preceptor and prophet. But the above examples should suffice to illustrate the historical connection and liberation, the foundation and development of the New Testament revelation brought by Jesus Christ.

The words to the Hebrews to the effect that God spoke definitively through his Son, and those of the Johannine Gospel that the Spirit leads the disciples to the whole truth,—these words remain true. New Testament revelation is eschatological, *non plus ultra,* warranted by the apostles, and recorded in essential content in the New Testament writing. But the subsequent centuries, in which the Church approaches her goal of fulfillment of salvation, are meaningful for revelation in another sense. A living, oral tradition is necessary for the safeguarding of the treasure of revelation, for the definition of its limits, for its explanation and clarification. God's eschatological revelation was announced within time and planted into history. It has been placed under the protection of the Church, and must be unlocked and made fruitful for every age and for every view of life. The salvific truth which Jesus brought to this earth, then, is not some implastic, dead greatness, but a living light which illuminates anew each moment of time and must ever be taken up anew by mankind.

3. THE ABSOLUTE CHARACTER OF BIBLICAL REVELATION

Although the word of God has entered into human language and history, it has not by that fact become a completely relative thing, for it had valid relevance not only for a particular age and a definite people, but "will stand for ever" (Is. 40, 8), as it continues to be the true revelation of the way of salvation throughout every historical and earthly change. The time-bound tenor of the biblical language, its ever-changing imagerial and idiomatic forms, are the ornaments of an unchanging eternal truth. We will here attempt to clarify the nature of this absolute character of biblical revelation with a few examples; though in so doing, we must always keep in mind the difference between Old and New Testament revelation.

The Old Testament, even as the New, contains absolute and final revelation. There is only *one* truth, the divine truth, which in itself is indivisible and not relative. What we must attempt to discern is what and how much God wanted to reveal at a given time. What has unchanging validity in the Old Testament revelation is what God disclosed to us about himself, his oneness and spirituality, his creation and maintenance of the world, as well as his saving plan for the redemption of mankind. The figurative ideas about creation in the Old Testament were to a large extent determined by the cosmology of the ancient world, but they nevertheless contain a pertinent message for us who live in a very different world and who have a very different cosmology: that God is separate from the material world, that in his divine providence he cares for men, that he brought the world into existence and sustains it in its existence. "By the word of the Lord the heavens were made, and all their host by the breath of his mouth" (Ps. 33, 6). "Let them praise the name of the Lord! For he commanded and they were created. And he established them for ever and ever; he fixed their bounds which cannot be passed" (Ps. 148, 5–6). God filled heaven and earth with his presence, he rules everything, and he knows all things (Ps. 139). "For the spirit of the Lord fills the world, is all-embracing, and knows man's utterance" (Wis. 1, 7). God watches over all of creation (Ps. 104).

Jesus takes it for granted, so to speak, that all of the basic teachings about God and creation in the Old Testament are true, and therefore he does not teach them anew, or as something new.

Even the election of the Israelite nation was not merely a for-the-moment and isolated deed on God's part, but rather was a decision which will never lose its power and meaning. Now salvation will no longer remain possible only for this small nation. The covenant with Israel was God's "tool" for implementing the final salvation of all peoples. Already among the ancient prophets this gathering of all nations was foretold (see the people's pilgrimage to Mount Zion: Is. 2; Mic. 4). By means of the new covenant the promise of salvation was only transposed onto a new level, that is, that salvation was made possible now for all peoples; and would be made possible once and for all, for all peoples, through the shedding of the blood of Jesus. Israel's role in the history of salvation is not repudiated by this new contract; rather, Israel and the gentiles are together formed into a new people of God, which will now be able to achieve its destiny. Not only has the Messiah risen out of Israel (see Jn. 4, 22), but his preëminence in salvation history is maintained in the New Testament (see Rom. 1, 16f.), and at the end his authorization is realized (see Rom. 11, 25f.). For ". . . it is not as though the word of God had failed" (Rom. 9, 6).

However, there are in the Old Testament divine revelations and instructions which were at one time limited by reason of their particular salvation-history context. This is especially true of those parts of God's law which were concerned with Israel's national life and worship. There was, at the time of the old covenant, and corresponding to its theocratic outlook, a great unity in all of God's laws and ordinances, since Israel's whole life was determined by God and his law. Thus, when the new covenant came to be made, many of God's laws which had been gathered together in the Torah lost all meaning.

Even so, Jesus, from the very beginning of his ministry, declared that he had not come to undo the law and the prophets, but to fulfill; that is, to progress, effect, and complete the history of salvation (see Mt. 5, 17). For this reason, many of God's laws which had meaning only because of the historical circumstances when they were given, and which had become outdated, were done away with. The good news of Jesus superseded the old laws in the sense that the latter were now "overhauled."

The New Testament contains also the unsurpassable revelation of God, completely developed in content. There is no new revelation above and beyond it. Even if, as we have seen, it was necessary that New Testament revelation be further developed, unlocked, adjusted to the respective understanding, it still remains the eschatological revelation of Jesus Christ. Of the promised Holy Spirit, the Paraclete, who was to direct this opening and unsealing of the revelation of Jesus, Jesus himself says: "He will glorify me, for he will take what is mine and declare it to you" (Jn. 16, 14). All salvation is determined and revealed in the cross and the resurrection of Jesus. "And there is salvation in no one else, for there is no other name under heaven given among men by which we must be saved" (Acts 4, 12). "The Son" is nothing but the revelation of the Father: he who sees him, sees also the Father (Jn. 14, 9). Thus it is that the words of

63

Jesus can only be brought again to mind, his salvific acts made present, made vital and fruitful in word and sacrament.

There is only one revelation to come, that is, the onset of the eschatological events. But if the New Testament calls this happening a revelation, it is not a new revelation as against that of Jesus Christ, but rather the unveiling, the actualization of that which Christ has foretold and promised. The Son of man who is to come is no other than he who once walked upon the earth; and his Parousia will only reveal him for who he really is: the Son of God upraised to the right hand of God and surrounded by power and glory.

We ourselves will only then become what we are now in obscurity; we will become revealed together with Christ in glory (see Col. 3, 4). The eschatological happening is therefore only the manifestation of that which is present but concealed in Christ, the appearance of whatever we have believed and hoped in but have not seen until that moment. "Beloved, we are God's children now; it does not yet appear what we shall be, but we know that when he appears we shall be like him, for we shall see him as he is" (1 Jn. 3, 2).

It is certainly true that the truth of New Testament revelation is "absolute" only insofar as it contains everything necessary unto salvation. All that has been said above concerning the salvific character of the truth prevails. There is no need for further revelation insofar as the way to salvation is pointed out and opened by Christ, so that we both know our goal and have the power to attain it. The early Church became aware of this when the first heretics wanted to go beyond the traditional Christian faith. Most clear are the words of 2 Jn. 9: "Any one who goes ahead and does not abide in the doctrine of Christ does not have God; he who abides in the doctrine has both the Father and the Son." This explains the warning of 1 Jn. 2, 24: "Let what you heard from the beginning abide in you." Similarly, the pastoral letters warn against heretics and their myths, against human ordinances and influences destructive of moral sense: these are characterized as people who "reject the truth" (Tit. 1, 14; see 1 Tim. 6, 5; 2 Tim. 2, 18, and elsewhere). In contrast, the Church is characterized as the stronghold of truth and of "healthy instruction"; the community of the living God is the "house of God," the "pillar and bulwark of the truth" (1 Tim. 3, 15). The words of God in Scripture are of particular significance: they ". . . are able to instruct you for salvation through faith in Jesus Christ" (2 Tim. 3, 25).

The revelation of the Son is the crown and summit of all divine revelation, the last Word of God to mankind, the Word of truth and of life, because the Son is the "pioneer of salvation," who is called and empowered to bring "many sons to glory" (Heb. 2, 10).

III.

Man Before God's Revealed Truth

"For the word of God is living and active, sharper than any two-edged sword, piercing to the division of soul and spirit, of joints and marrow, and discerning the thoughts and intentions of the heart. And before him no creature is hidden, but all are open and laid bare to the eyes of him with whom we have to do" (Heb. 4, 12–13).

God's word and truth are different from human words and human truth. They are piercing, demanding, and they place man in a position of decision. Today we have more fully realized this character of biblical revelation (though it has always possessed it), and it is a valuable fruit of existential thinking. What God proclaims and allows to be proclaimed is never without a demand for a response on our part. In the Bible, all truth is not truth for its own sake, but for men; it is an historically promulgated word for an historically situated mankind. The word of God speaks to each man, the contemporary man, personally and individually; it is a crucial word, for it puts man into the crisis of judgment. Man is responsible for his future salvation, for whether he will be saved or damned; and he acts out his life under judgment of God's word, which comes to him as God's revealed truth. The word of God in the Letter to the Hebrews will not at a later time say something different from what it said in the beginning, when it was written; what man must do is to learn the meaning of the words, to learn what was intended by God, then as now.

1. THE "ESCHATOLOGICAL" CHARACTER OF REVELATION

A new "eschatological" concept of revelation has lately developed in theology and exegesis; briefly, it is that the revelation of Jesus Christ is to be understood as a decisive, ever contemporary address to man, God's existential demand upon him which requires of him decision and commitment. Bultmann has presented this character of revelation in a very impressive if one-sided way: "Revelation is not an explanation, a piece of information, but an event . . . Therefore, the revelation directly confronting us must be for us a continuing event."* The things which take place in revelation, Bultmann continues, "will only be understood if they are seen as taking place in the present, in our own present."†

"Eschatological," then, is no longer interpreted to mean in reference to future events in the last days of time, but

---

* "The Concept of Revelation in the New Testament," p. 78.
† *Ibid.*, p. 79.

rather in reference to a present decision which will determine the future, since it will decide a man's salvation or damnation.

This interpretation based on existential theology is justified by the message of the New Testament insofar as Jesus, and his disciples after him, do not simply foretell the future, but also report a present condition: God is ready—God is about to grant grace and mercy to those who hear the word, who convert and believe. The events of the future are not something distant, outside of myself, having no relation to me, no bearing on my situation. Rather, they make demands on me here and now, imposing the most vital decisions about myself. The historicity of man is here taken very seriously, for historicity consists in the fact that man must determine his own future. In view of revelation, however, man does not have absolute power over himself, but must face up to the situation of decision provided by God. The word of God, like a keen double-edged sword, penetrates him to the very heart, leaving him no choice save acceptance or rejection, belief or unbelief—and therewith, salvation or damnation.

It was Jesus, in fact, who placed man into this position of direct personal decision. His eschatological message becomes a present challenge, the time of his activity becomes the crisis, the eschatological *kairos*. ". . . When you see a cloud rising in the west, you say at once, 'A shower is coming'; and so it happens. And when you see the south wind blowing, you say, 'There will be scorching heat'; and it happens. You hypocrites! You know how to interpret the appearance of earth and sky; but why do you not know how to interpret the present time [*kairos*]?" (Lk. 12, 54ff.). "As it was in the days of Noah, so will it be in the days of the Son of man. They ate, they drank, they married, they were given in marriage, until the day when Noah entered the ark, and the flood came and destroyed them all. Likewise it was in the days of Lot—they ate, they drank, they bought, they sold, they planted, they built, but on the day when Lot went out from Sodom fire and brimstone rained from heaven and destroyed them all—so will it be on the day when the Son of man is revealed" (Lk. 17, 26–30). All of Jesus' sermons were as prophetically pressing as these words; they demanded instant conversion, and faith in the message of salvation.

St. John the evangelist understood this demanding character of Jesus' message and expressed it in his own way. Rightly has a "realized eschatology" been attributed to him. He spoke of the promise of "eternal life" to those who already believed, but he transferred the judgment to the present. "He who believes in the Son has eternal life; he who does not obey the Son shall not see life, but the wrath of God rests upon him" (Jn. 3, 36). "He who believes in him is not condemned; he who does not believe is condemned already, because he has not believed in the name of the only Son of God" (Jn. 3, 18). Towards the end of his ministry, Jesus summarized some of the things he had often spoken about: "He who rejects me and does not receive my sayings has a judge; the word that I have spoken will be his judge on the last day" (Jn. 12, 48).

On the basis of the "eschatological" characteristics of Jesus' message (the *kerygma*), one certainly may not deny the future eschatological events, but, for John, these events attain their full meaning for the individual here and now. He finds it depressing that the "world" remains closed to the saving news of its divine, eschatological revealer, Jesus Christ. "And this is the judgment, that the light has come into the world, and men loved darkness rather than light, because their deeds were evil" (Jn. 3, 19). "But to all who received him, who believed in his name, he gave power to become children of God" (Jn. 1, 12). The Gospel of St. John is an excellent example of how the words once spoken by Jesus can resound to new depths and speak ever anew to men; but, at basis, the entire New Testament is a witness to the decisive nature of the Gospel.

The passage from the Letter to the Hebrews which immediately precedes the introductory phrase of the present chapter provides an excellent example of the "eschatological" address of God's word. Here Psalm 95, which once referred to the people of Israel, refers now to the new people of God, actually speaking to them, warning them of their situation. St. Paul admonishes the community once strong in faith, but becoming now a little lame in zeal, by holding up to them the "typical" example of the generation in the wilderness, which did not heed the leadership of God, but grumbled and rebelled against him. And God cast away that generation of the wilderness, as a forewarning to future generations. "Therefore, as the Holy Spirit says, 'Today, when you hear his voice, do not harden your hearts as in the rebellion, on the day of testing in the wilderness, where your fathers put me to the test and saw my works for forty years'" (Heb. 3, 7ff.).

The Psalms make present to ancient Israel the events in the wilderness, the behavior of the fathers and the response of God; but now it becomes an urgent admonition to the hearers, who are members of the new people of God. "Take care, brethren, lest there be in any of you an evil, unbelieving heart, leading you to fall away from the living God. But exhort one another every day, as long as it is called 'today,' that none of you may be hardened by the deceitfulness of sin" (Heb. 3, 12f.). "Every day," "today": this is the present situation of decision. This is the critical hour which determines our whole future salvation. "For good news came to us just as to them; but the message which they heard did not benefit them, because it did not meet with faith in the hearers" (Heb. 4, 2). The new people of God receive anew the promise of "rest," but the new hearers of the promise must heed the word: today, when you hear his voice, do not harden your hearts.

The entire New Testament resounds with this eschatological "today," beginning with the declaration of Jesus that in him Scripture is fulfilled (Lk. 4, 21), and continuing up to the apostolic exhortation. "For he says, 'At the acceptable time I have listened to you, and helped you on the day of salvation.' Behold, now is the acceptable time; behold, now is the day of salvation" (2 Cor. 6, 2). And again, there is the admonition to "[make] the most of the time [as wise men]" (Eph. 5, 16).

Christ stands in the time of salvation, it is true; but he does not yet possess salvation undisputably and consummately. Christian existence is suspended between today and tomorrow, between the first and the final stages of salvation. As St. Paul succinctly puts it: ". . . in this hope we were saved" (Rom. 8, 24).

Even Christ is constantly called upon to effect his salvation, to actualize by moral confirmation the salvation bestowed on him. We are graciously saved by God, by reason of the salvific action of Christ. But this salvation is provisional: we are saved in hope, to the extent that we allow the grace of God to affect us. It is at this point of our salvation history that the word of God unceasingly concerns us: ". . . God was in Christ reconciling the world to himself, . . . We beseech you on behalf of Christ, be reconciled to God" (2 Cor. 5, 19f.). We receive God's word of reconciliation in the announcement, and it becomes for us an admonition. We must answer to every word which reveals to us God's eschatological mercy: we are responsible for every word.

2. THE "EXISTENTIAL" CHARACTER OF REVELATION

As man perceives the intent and demand of the word of revelation in this way, he obtains a profound insight into his own human essence, which is most important for his self-comprehension. In faith, man's entire existence becomes illumined; he sees himself before God and can no longer envision himself in any other context save in this confrontation with God. Here we have what is perhaps the paramount meaning of revelation: the personal encounter of man with his God, which is brought about by God himself in his revelation and in his demands that man make a response. This we may call the "existential" character of revelation. We will examine this mark of revelation at closer range by inquiring into the self-comprehension of man in face of the call of revelation, in the perfection of faithful existence, and of the faithful man's understanding of the world.

Man's Understanding of Existence in the Light of Revelation

The revelational event, as the word of truth directed towards us, makes possible a new comprehension of our own human existence. It questions the previous self-understanding of man, that is, of man left to his own resources. Natural man can apprehend his existence only as "existence unto death."

73

The man who believes in Christ, on the other hand, knows himself a part of God's life, knows himself called to eternal life in communion with God. On a new, elevated plane, we reclaim ourselves: we believe, and this faith gives new direction and new content to our existence.

The man who depends on himself alone, who seeks only himself, who measures himself by his own standard: he is doomed to failure, he is "lost." This comes to the fore in Jesus' unvarnished speech, for in his eyes every man is a sinner, and for this reason liable unto the judgment of God and unto everlasting death. On the report that a number of Galileans had been put to death by Pilate while they were sacrificing in the temple, Jesus comments: "Do you think that these Galileans were worse sinners than all the other Galileans, because they suffered thus? I tell you, No; but unless you repent you will all likewise perish" (Lk. 13, 1ff.). He does not speak here of sudden death, of physical destruction, but of the actual destruction, the everlasting death which threatens the sinner. The last and most terrible thing is not physical death, but rather the utter destruction of existence which comes from God: "And do not fear those who kill the body but cannot kill the soul; rather fear him who can destroy both soul and body in hell" (Mt. 10, 28). The word "soul" is rather inadequate to express what is really meant here, namely, that genuine life of man which has been given him by God, and which can be taken away. It is that most interior life, indestructible by earthly powers, which man possesses in common with God. Jesus refers to this life with the paradox, ". . . whoever would save his life will lose it, and whoever loses his life for my sake will find it" (Mt. 16, 25). This is also the sense of the often misinterpreted phrase, ". . . what will it profit a man, if he gains the whole world and forfeits his life?" (Mt. 16, 26). Such statements are founded on the conviction that human existence is greater and more profound than all other life on earth.

Although man is bound to the physical and animal levels of existence, he transcends these levels in his personal, spiritual existence and participates in the purely spiritual life of God. The comprehension of the totality of human "being" hinges on the perception of that nucleus of the question of human existence. If he misunderstands the ultimate meaning of existence, his being-in-communion-with-God, man is destroyed, annihilated. And man himself accomplishes this self-annihilation through rebellion against God, through sin. Scripture has it that he becomes liable unto the wrath and the judgment of God. Man achieves the true goal of human existence only if God pardons him, receives him back into his community, restores him to divine life.

These things can be understood only in faith—they are too deep for human reason. But they were familiar thoughts to the religious men of Jesus' time, who lived in the centuries-old tradition of revelation. And so they could under-

75

stand the words of Jesus, "Your sins are forgiven," or "Your faith has saved you; go in peace" (Lk. 7, 48. 50).

In the well-known Chapter 7 of the Letter to the Romans, St. Paul describes the hopeless, desolate plight of a man dependent on himself, and unredeemed. Despite his most earnest effort, this man is unable to accomplish the good which he so fervently desires to do. He is dominated by sin, the tyrannical power which possesses him. "Wretched man that I am! Who will deliver me from this body of death?" (Rom. 7, 24).

The Christian teaching about salvation can be understood only against this somber background of man unable by his own power to free himself from entanglement in sin and the decay of death. This awareness is brought to the fore in St. John's dualistic portrayal of "darkness" and "light," of "death" and "life." Unbelieving, sinful man moves about in darkness; ". . . if any one walks in the night, he stumbles, because the light is not in him" (Jn. 11, 10). "But he who hates his brother is in the darkness and walks in the darkness, and does not know where he is going, because the darkness has blinded his eyes" (1 Jn. 2, 11).

This dark and hopeless situation of man is reversed only when he approaches the "light," that is, the revealer Jesus Christ. "I am the light of the world; he who follows me will not walk in darkness, but will have the light of life" (Jn. 8, 12). "Walk while you have the light, lest the darkness overtake you; he who walks in the darkness does not know where he goes. While you have the light, believe in the light, that you may become sons of light" (Jn. 12, 35f.). In faith is effected the transition from the sphere of darkness and of death into the realm of light and of life. ". . . he who hears my word and believes him who sent me, has eternal life; he does not come into judgment, but has passed from death to life" (Jn. 5, 24).

Through faith in the eschatological ambassador from God, through union with this only real bringer of light and of salvation, man achieves a new existence, a faithful existence "in Christ." St. Paul speaks of a new creation: "Therefore, if any one is in Christ, he is a new creation; the old has passed away, behold, the new has come" (2 Cor. 5, 17).

Now this new God-given existence shapes man's understanding of himself: ". . . it is no longer I who live, but Christ who lives in me; and the life I now live in the flesh I live by faith in the Son of God, who loved me and gave himself for me" (Gal. 2, 20). This fresh view of self in faith is therefore not merely a new recognition which man of himself wins through faith, but it is rather the result and fruit of the new God-given existence. In this new existence we discover our humanness to be entirely dependent on God, elevated by the mercy of God, redeemed, fulfilled. In this salvific revelation God becomes not only our companion, but also our redeemer.

God bestows the newness of life out of pure love, and as

a consequence the disposition of the Christian is fundamentally one of gratitude and joy, of peace and confidence. "Therefore, since we are justified by faith, we have peace with God through our Lord Jesus Christ" (Rom. 5, 1). "In this is love perfected in us, that we may have confidence for the day of judgment, . . . There is no fear in love, but perfect love casts out fear" (1 Jn. 4, 17f.). Thus is banished the fear which governs "being unto death," overcome by the union with God who is the source of life.

This new understanding of existence will certainly not be assimilated fully and realized by all the faithful. Since it is a part of the salvation-revelation of Jesus Christ, however, Christian preaching must aim at making it actual and reflexive for the faithful.

The Understanding of the World in the Light of Revelation

The new Christian self-comprehension in faith also effects a change in our relation to the world. The world is not a domain, in our service, amidst which we flourish and find fulfillment. It, too, stands now in the light of the question of salvation: How shall I be able to find God and salvation in the world in which I live, and together with the world which I make use of, and through the world which I traverse?

The revelational meaning of "the world" is twofold. On

the one hand, the word signifies the creation of God entrusted to man that he might cultivate and govern it. On the other, it refers to an historically unfolding force into whose destiny historically existing man is drawn. Under this latter aspect, the world before and the world distant from Christ are seen to be in a deplorable condition: darkened by sin, perverted, in a desperate state of development towards annihilation. But through redemption in Christ it has regained the hope and the conviction that it has been called unto the glory, the re-creation of all things, unto a new and transfigured state.

The New Testament concept of "world" is many-sided and often difficult to define. It was certainly influenced by the pessimistic and dualistic view then prevalent. It might seem at first glance that the New Testament authors do not do justice to the "goodness" of God's creation. But the world of creation in its pristine state of perfection is never disavowed. It is just that the "world" in its historical shape, that is, the world as a history known to man—a history perverted by wickedness and sin—is brought strongly to the fore. "Do not love the world or the things in the world. If any one loves the world, love for the father is not in him. For all that is in the world, the lust of the flesh and the lust of the eyes and the pride of life, is not of the father but is of the world" (1 Jn. 15f.). This passage clearly takes a moral view of the world, a religious view of the hazards which threaten man if he becomes too involved with material goods

and human values. In this context also we must understand
the words of the apostle James: ". . . friendship with the
world means enmity with God" (4, 4). This is a warning
against excessive involvement with worldly business which
can too easily make a man forget the service of God. Fundamentally, this is what Jesus means when he says: "No one
can serve two masters; for either he will hate the one and
love the other, or he will be devoted to the one and despise
the other. You cannot serve God and mammon" (Mt. 6, 24).

It is undeniable that the New Testament takes a reserved
view of the world as a perilous and enticing power in the
face of this religious aspect of the service of God. But it
would be gravely to misinterpret the message of Jesus were
one to conclude from this a fundamental "rejection of the
world," even less a "flight from the world."

The relation of Christians to the world according to the
New Testament is circumspectly examined by R. Völkl in
*The Christian and the World According to the New Testa-
ment.** For the teaching of Jesus he sets up a dialectic oppo-
sition between abnegation and affirmation of the world.
"The emphasis of the moral demand of Jesus is placed on
the abnegation of the world. This is to be understood, however, in the sense of an 'aversion,' that is to say, a turning
away from the spirit of this world and towards the essentially eschatological reign of God. If the negative attitude
towards worldly possessions is most prominent, this must

* Würzburg, 1961.

not be taken in effect as the rejection of this or that specific material object, but as self-denial, as the triumph over 'worldliness.' . . . There is a limited 'yes' to the goods and accouterments of this age, but interest does not revolve about 'world improvement,' progress, and secular reform. What is essential is the affirmation of the world in the sense of a universal love for the 'world of man' and for the Christian mission. It is this very love for the world which prohibits flight from the world" (p. 153). We must understand the purely religious intent of Jesus, or we will falsely conclude that he denigrates worldly goods, or that he is not sensitive to the meaning of family and professional life, or of state and industry, law and culture. If Jesus does not specifically refer to these matters nor comment on their positive values, it is only because he consciously limits himself to his religious mission and message. At the same time his own behavior—he comports himself with natural ease in the society and culture of his time—sufficiently indicates that he does not want to alienate men from their worldly tasks. Moreover, his words frequently demonstrate his affirmation of the divinely created world and of the workaday world of man.

For the Christian in his religious view of existence, the world is certainly a duality. On the one hand, it is the locus of his mastery both of his secular duties and of his ultimate salvation. On the other hand, it can become an obstacle in his way towards God. The Christian is therefore perpetually caught up in the tension between affirmation and abnegation of the world. While he must not "be conformed to this world" (Rom. 12, 2), he must "deal with the world," but "as though [he] had no dealings with it" (1 Cor. 7, 31).

It is possible that some of these warnings are historically limited, are to be understood in terms of the Christian situation in the world at that time. But rather than examine that possibility, we shall here simply mark the fact that the Christian is required to become "desecularized" in view of his new existence in Christ, of his having been made a citizen of heaven, of his gravitation towards the eschatological goal. So far from removing or alienating him from his earthly tasks, this desecularization provides him with the inner freedom to overcome the "world."

This Christian understanding of the world and relation to the world which is fundamental, historico-eschatological, and therefore in a constant state of tension, is utterly independent of the variable scientific world-view. The biblical image of the external world, which surely has been revamped, does not encroach upon the revelational teaching concerning the world as such, that is, as a force relevant to the religious and moral demeanor of man. As the biblical predicates on God and creation are independent of the respective scientific discoveries, just so is the biblically ordained behavior in and attitude towards the world not—or, not decisively—influenced by the changing circumstances of the historical world as we experience it. To be sure,

82

technical advances always create new questions as to the deportment of the Christian in his life and his profession; to be sure, contemporary society ever gives rise to additional problems which the Christian must solve in the context of his membership in the community. But these changes do not affect basically his behavior before the face of God as prescribed by the Bible. In fact, he must, conversely, apply the religious directives of revelation to his own historical condition, translate them corresponding to the altered situation, and make personal decisions in the spirit of the Bible.

The biblical formulas for the old world-view do not force us to a radical "demythologizing." On the other hand, the revelational content of the Bible obliges us to reëvaluate that world-view to the extent that it ranges beyond the physical and requires us to determine our behavior towards the world and towards life.

Revelation challenges an autonomous, secularized world-view; and the mere encounter of the Christian with the world—that is, with the particular world in which he is historically present—is accomplished in the light of revelation and the view-of-existence which it presents.

3. THE SIGNIFICANCE OF DIVINE REVELATION FOR MANKIND

The above discussion should have made it clear that revelation places man squarely before God. The revealing God addresses man, turning to him as a companion—and demands of him the response of faith. And he who hears the word of God is drawn into the community of God.

We see, then, that revelation is no mere monologue of God, but a proclamation which becomes dialogue when man answers in faith and "performs" God's truth. We should by now be aware of the meaning for man of this personal-dialogic process. As the unveiling of divine truth and the instant message to man, revelation requires that every man decide how he is to understand himself, and how he is to comport himself in the world. Before God, the absolute Being and the ultimate Value, man must opt to use himself as the standard for all things and the norm for all behavior, or, on the other hand, to submit himself to God and bend to his holy will. Man must determine whether he will be his own master or choose God for his Master; whether he will regulate his own world or subordinate his world to the disposition of God; whether he will choose his own future autonomously or relegate it to the judgment of God.

God does not deprive man of freedom. In fact, he accords him genuine freedom to conquer himself by foregoing the questionable freedom of choosing evil. The redemption in Christ, which man accepts through faith, liberates him from enslavement to the powers of sin and death, and brings him to a new service in true moral freedom (see Gal. 5, 1. 13).

The question remains: What is the significance of this revelation of the divine truth of salvation for mankind as such? According to the Bible, the answer would be that only through revelation does man attain his central and sovereign position in the created world, or, more correctly, he regains it after his falling away from the original vocation.

The accounts of creation—each in its own way—express this primacy and sovereignty of man. The oldest, most strongly anthropological representation runs: ". . . then the Lord God formed man of dust from the ground, and breathed into his nostrils the breath of life; and man became a living being" (Gen. 1, 7). Man is here represented as the central point of creation, and as intimately bound to the earth—this is recognized immediately from the play on the words *adam* ("man") and *adamah* ("earth"). But man's existence derives from God who inspires him with the breath of life. This emphasis on the direct creation of man at the same time points up his unique and privileged status in creation.

The following account of the situation in paradise underlines this axial position of man: God puts paradise at the disposal of man. Keeping him under his divine care, he also sets him under his divine law. According to Gen. 1, man is the last and greatest creature of God, having dominion over the earth: and most important, he is made in the image and likeness of God. "So God created man in his own image, in the image of God he created him; male and female he created them" (Gen. 1, 27). Man himself by his fall has darkened this Godlikeness, which is renewed and restored to original brilliance only through the redemptive act of Christ. According to St. Paul, we "... have put off the old nature with its practices and have put on the new nature, which is being renewed in knowledge after the image of its creator" (Col. 3, 9f.). Man again becomes the crown of creation, and the sign of the new, perfected creation: for redeemed man is intimately united to Christ the second Adam, the founder of a new humanity, the witness and guarantor of the world to come. For creation—liable to annihilation, to servility, to destruction—"waits with eager longing for the revealing of the sons of God" and "the glorious liberty of the children of God" (Rom. 8, 19. 21).

The Bible, then, is anthropologically oriented, with regard to creation as well as to redemption and to the expectation of the world to come. To the scientific way of thinking, this world-view which opens with man and focuses on man appears strange and inadequate. Man seems to have shrunken to the size of a ludicrous dwarf who takes himself far too seriously, by contrast with the stupendous scale of the universe as modern astronomy reveals it, and by contrast with the potential lying dormant in the cosmos and yet untapped by astrophysicism. And yet, is it not true that man is and remains an exceptional being in his capacity to grasp and pentrate his environment, to comprehend the world as such? Does not that which we call "universe" become a unified whole only in the very fact of being apprehended by man? Without an unwarranted shift from the plane of induction theory to that of ontology, there still remains the question of the unique situation and capacity of man to exercise his sovereign office in the cosmos.

To this question the seemingly simplistic terminology of the Bible gives a profound reply: "When I look at thy heavens, the work of thy fingers, the moon and the stars which thou hast established; what is man that thou art mindful of him, and the son of man that thou dost care for him? Yet thou hast made him little less than God, and dost crown him with glory and honor. Thou hast given him dominion over the works of thy hands; thou hast put all things under his feet, . . ." (Ps. 8, 3ff.). Even if the ancient world-view did not consider the possibility of life on other planets, the answer of religion persists: man's lowliness and his magnitude; his minuteness in proportion to the immensity of the universe and his grandeur by virtue of his proximity to God; his physical insignificance and his God-given dignity.

Our age is flooded with scientific discoveries and intoxicated by technical success. At the same time, we are in danger of addiction to materialistic ways of thinking and the loss of genuinely "human" feeling. In view of this danger, biblical revelation is of a significance which cannot be overestimated. For divine revelation is far more than a personal message to each man: even more is it an unmistakable appeal to the whole of mankind. There is a heightened urgency for today in the words of a cultural philosopher at the beginning of our century: "We have won a world and lost the soul" (R. Eucken, *Der Wahrheitsgehalt der Religion,* p. 43). H. Sedlmayr, in mid-century, called this the "loss of the mean." At stake is the salvation of man who, without the revealed divine truth, is hopelessly lost in the world which he has himself fashioned and experienced.

Other problems are relevant here: the equality of all men without regard to sex, race, social position; the peaceful coexistence of nations by abstention from conquest and war; the foundations of justice and political organization, and the like. These considerations are certainly relevant even in the area of strictly humanitarian ethics: but particularly in the domain of morality, man is most profoundly committed to biblically revealed religion which confronts him inevitably with God and his judgment. No man, no state, no power on earth can alter or abolish the holy will of God revealed by Jesus Christ. Here, all men and all nations must submit to a superior law which serves unto order and peace on earth. God's truth is more steadfast than any law of man or any power in the world.

We must, finally, consider a matter of key import under the present dark circumstances, in view of man's terror of the unleashing of atomic power: the path into the future and the meaning of history. If we had not revelation, the course of history might appear to us senseless, at the mercy of the whim of man; we would tremble at the thought of the agglomeration of power, and lose all hope in the future of mankind. Or we might fall prey to perilous ideologies which entice us with the thought of an unattainable paradise on earth, a utopia which would prove a nightmare.

It is the conviction of the Bible that God is the Lord of history in spite all of man's deliberation and planning, in spite of all political power, in spite of all obscurity. Tiny Israel harbored this confidence amidst oppression at the hands of powerful nations. "Behold, the nations are like a drop from a bucket, and are accounted as the dust on the scales; behold he takes up the isles like fine dust. . . . All the nations are as nothing before him, they are accounted by him as less than nothing and emptiness" (Is. 40, 15. 17).

The New Testament is filled with the solid hope in the future kingdom promised by Christ. The most eloquent witness of this is St. John's Book of Revelation. Its language and imagery might be historically conditioned, and its visions and phantasms might appear to us fantastic. And yet its religious attitude and expectation remain constant, and its predications for the future—if we realize its actual intention—are a part of the divine truth of revelation.

The motif of the book appears in the heavenly paeans of triumph which ring out even amidst the greatest affliction of the human community. "Great and wonderful are thy deeds, O Lord God the Almighty! Just and true are thy ways, O King of the ages! Who shall not fear and glorify thy name, O Lord? For thou alone art holy. All nations come and worship thee, for thy judgments have been revealed" (Rev. 15, 3f.). The rulers and nations hostile to God take up with a vengeance a last-ditch attack: but in the end Christ is victorious. ". . . he will rule them with a rod of iron; he will tread the wine press of the fury of the wrath of God the Almighty. On his robe and on his thigh he has a name inscribed, King of kings and Lord of lords" (Rev. 19, 15f.). These are but images, enriched by the age-old language and rhetoric of the Bible. And yet they express the biblical theology of history: above all forces and powers which drive history onward, there stands the Lord God who in the end achieves his aim, fulfilling his promise and establishing his kingdom which is not of this world but of the next.

Again, it is the conviction of the Bible that the word of divine revelation is not only true but also irreversibly and irresistibly effective. Men are to hear and heed the word of revelation, and yet revelation prevails against all human resistance. "For my thoughts are not your thoughts, neither are your ways my ways, says the Lord. For as the heavens are higher than the earth, so are my ways higher than your ways and my thoughts than your thoughts. For as the rain and the snow come down from heaven, and return not thither but water the earth, making it bring forth and sprout, giving seed to the sower and bread to the eater, so shall my word be that goes forth from my mouth; it shall not return to me empty, but it shall accomplish that which

90

I purpose, and prosper in the thing for which I sent it" (Is. 55, 8ff.).

We have been considering the "truth which makes us free," the truth of biblical revelation. We have discovered in the Bible a concept of truth different from that of philosophy, of science, even of daily life: a concept of truth proceeding out of the existence and reality of God.

Revelation transforms the abstract divine truth into actuality. Revelation introduces us to the thought of God, directs us towards the divine will for our salvation—and points the way to the attainment of that salvation. Revelation accosts each one of us immediately, personally, here and now, and demands a decision. Revelation answers for us, for all mankind, the question of our existence on this earth, a question in the face of which we would otherwise stand hopeless and perplexed.

The divine eschatological ambassador, God's own Son Jesus Christ, asserts that the truth will make us free. Have we any choice but to accept in faith the truth of revelation and "hold fast to the word of life" (Phil. 2, 16)?

IV.

The Concept of Revelation in the Bible

THE Bible, which for the Christian faith is simply the book of revelation, is continually a source of new problems for theology in its attempt to understand revelation. This hinges on the fact that every theological trend develops a particular concept of revelation and—insofar as it wants to be called Christian—must be verified in the Bible, while at the same time bringing into focus anew whatever truths we encounter as "revelation" through or in the Bible. Every theologian, taking for granted a certain foreknowledge about revelation, examines those documents of the Christian faith and seeks in them a complete and clear answer. The Bible does not employ any uniform and limited terminology for divine revelation,[1] but rather presents a particular event, its conse-

---

[1] For a survey of inconsistent terminology in the Old Testament, see H. Haag, " 'Offenbaren' in der hebräischen Bibel," in *TZBas* 16, 1960, pp. 251–258; in the New Testament, see H. Schulte, *Der Begriff der Offenbarung im Neuen Testament,* München, 1949, pp. 34–84. See also the individual key words in *TWNT*: "γνωρίζω," I, 718 (R. Bultmann); "δηλόω," II, pp. 60f. (R. Bultmann); "ἀποχαλύπτω," III, pp. 565–597 (A. Oepke, main article on "Revelation"). The key words "φανερόω" and "ἐμφανίζω" are still lacking.

quences and meaning, through various techniques of expression, and does not, therefore, exclude the possibility of a changing mode of expression in the course of time. Looking at the history of theology since the Enlightenment we easily recognize the many past and present interpretations of that which the Bible witnesses alone by its existence but also by its definitive declarations. The rationalistic understanding of revelation, born out of the effort to delimit religion by the "boundaries of mere reason," faded in the Romantic age before irrational concepts based on emotion and inner experience. Such concepts remain alive to this day among groups which emphasize religious "experience" or "awakening." This tendency gave way to other vapid approaches which compared biblical revelation with similar claims of other religions, likening it to them or only relatively raising it above them. Against such liberal views, dialectical, existential theology emphasizes the unique, incomprehensible, shocking word of God, or comprehends revelation as an existential operation between God and man, and as the existential eschatological message of God to man, but nothing more. The task of leading us back again to a genuine biblical mentality is left to salvation-history theology. Without doubt, we today are turning our attention more and more to those basic underlying question, for the science of exegesis is more theologically oriented than ever before. The First Vatican Council found it necessary to clarify in a separate chapter[2]

[2] Session III, Chapter 2 (Denzinger, 1785–1788).

the Catholic belief with regard to revelation, and Vatican II renewed this theme in its *Constitution on Divine Revelation*. The following lines will in no way take a definite stand on the questions in this whole complex of problems, but will only bring to attention a few of the aspects which came to the fore in the renewed discussions, and try to clarify them to some extent from the viewpoint of the Catholic exegete.

1. REVELATION AND HISTORY

In order to gain access to the biblical understanding of revelation and an objective outlook on its concepts (contained in the Bible without a set terminology), it would be advisable to turn to the Letter to the Hebrews, which quite properly appears towards the end of the Bible since it both summarizes and clarifies the witnessing of the Bible both in detailed and as a whole: "In many and various ways God spoke of old to our fathers by the prophets; but in these last days he has spoken to us by a Son . . ." (1, 1f.). Each individual phrase has its own significance and ought to be examined if only in brief:

(a) ". . . *God* spoke . . ." Revelation is self-disclosure on the part of God, a communication from God. The Greek participial construction "ὁδεὸς λαλήσας . . . ἐλάλησεν" gives greater emphasis than the English translation to the initiative, the sovereign determination, the self-empowered action of God. This condescension and historical association of God

94

with man is something completely different from the human self-elevation sought by the mystics and the Gnostics, in mysteries and magic, to obtain admission to the hidden world of God, and thereby to find revelation.[3]

(b) ". . . God *spoke* . . ." The Bible can certainly describe in various ways God's stepping forth from his transcendence in order to encounter man and to communicate with him. However, the most frequent and most suitable word used to express this idea is the "speaking" of God, since it reflects most appropriately (according to human analogy) the spiritual self-disclosure and the transmission of the divine thought—this in contrast to those extra-biblical, human "revelations" which are believed to be obtained by "seeing."[4] It is also clear that the concern here is not for the natural revelation of God in his creation (see Rom. 1, 19f.: ἐφανέρωσεν).

(c) "In many and various ways . . ." Biblical revelation does not only take place in a divinely granted encounter of man with God, but it also has its own history. God has often and variously opened himself up to man. The Greek rhetorical mode of expression portrays the manifold shape of histor-

---

[3] In this context, see the well-documented study of A.-J. Festugière, *La révélation d'Hermès Trismégiste I: L'astrologie et les sciences occultes*, Paris, 1950, pp. 309–362. It is significant that here (as well as in the hermetical and other Gnostic texts) the biblical expressions for "revealing" are supressed.

[4] See W. Michaelis, "ὁράω," in *TWNT* V, pp. 323f.

ical appearances[5] and indicates in detail the great number of those who receive and who mediate revelation ($\pi o\lambda v\mu\rho\tilde{\omega}s$), as well as the means of revelation ($\pi o\lambda v\tau\xi\acute{o}\pi\omega s$): words, dreams, visions, symbolic actions. God has many ways of revealing himself and his thought to man and he has repeatedly made use of them.

(d) "... of old to our fathers ..." From the standpoint of the New Testament eschatological revelation, then, there is a past history to be looked back upon, a time gone by. But the expression "the fathers"—which was crystallized into a definite concept among the Jews and was taken up by primitive Christianity—makes us conscious of the fact that this past also bears a relation to the present, and is therefore not simply an "historical" past, but rather a past which affects and finds fulfillment in the future. Revelation history, despite its multiplicity, is meaningful and purposive. We can distinguish between the days "of old" of "the fathers"[6] and "these last days" in which "we" live as the eschatological people of God (see Heb. 3, 7—4, 11), but we cannot separate them, for, between that time of promise and this time of fulfillment, there is a real inner cohesion, and it follows that revelation is a unity, a cohesive entity, a culmination, so that all the steps and layers of the process of history bear him who stands at the summit. (We find the same

[5] See the linguistic parallels in H. Windisch, *Der Hebräerbrief*, second ed., Tübingen, 1931.

[6] See G. Schrenk in *TWNT* V, pp. 975–977.

contrast between "our fathers" and "us"—the eschatological generation—in 1 Cor. 10, 1-11.)

(e) "... by the prophets ..." The preceding will be made more clear by this phrase which characterizes all the mediators of revelation in the entire Old Testament. Their eyes were turned towards the fulfillment of salvation which has now become reality in the Son, as Peter accurately comments in 1 Pet. 1, 10f.: "The prophets who prophesied of the grace that was to be yours searched and inquired about this salvation; they inquired what person or time was indicated by the Spirit of Christ within them." By this it is made clear— entirely independent of whether or not the same is suggested by the preposition "ἐν" in Heb. 1, 1[7]—that God empowered and stirred up the prophets to make revelation through his *Spirit* so that the Spirit and not the human voice is the true mediator of revelation. According to 1 Pet. 1, 11, this is no other than the "Spirit of Christ," the preëxisting Christ himself (see 1 Cor. 10, 4).[8] Thus the eschatological ordering and the Christological centering of all revelation receives the strongest emphasis.

(f) "... in these last days ..." Here the eschatological awareness breaks through with a familiar phrase (the "last

[7] See O. Michel, *Der Brief an die Hebräer* (H. A. W. Meyers Komm. XIII eighth ed.), Göttingen, 1949. With good reason, he considers the instrumental ἐν to be the more probable; the prophets are mediators of revelation.

[8] This is the justifiable opinion (against newer explanations) of K. H. Schelkle, in *Die Petrusbriefe, der Judasbrief*, Freiburg i. Br., 1961, pp. 41f. The Fathers, too, were familiar with this thought (see *ibid.*, p. 41, note 3).

days"), for "these" days are those in which "we" live, and they are also the eschatological days (both meanings are covered by the one phrase). The New Testament revelation which came from the "Son" is the "last" one, the one towards which is oriented all of God's revelation, even that which "of old" was given to "the fathers." *Proton* and *eschaton* both are present in the Son's revelation, as is made clear in the following words concerning the Son: God has made him the heir of the universe just as he created the aeons through him. And yet this eschatological revelation is recorded in history (ἐλάλησεν:); it is both historical and eschatological.

(g) "... to us ..." This is said first of all by way of contrast to the "fathers"; further, it illustrates "these last days," in which the Son appeared, and to live in which is a grace and a blessing; but the phrase means even more. For in the dative construction of the speaking "to us" and to "the fathers" is found the *allocution* of the revealing God to man: man is visited by the word of God and is enjoined to listen and to obey, to believe and to act. God's speaking and self-disclosure is always directed towards man: it presupposes a listening ear and proceeds to say something which is at once promising and binding. St. Paul in the Letter to the Hebrews reminds his readers of this fact so that he may confront them here and now in their situation in his "word of exhortation" (13, 22), that is, in his preaching, with the revealed word of God which "is living and active, sharper

98

than any two-edged sword" (4, 12). He gives a gripping example of this in his homily on Psalm 95 which he introduces with the words: "Therefore, as the Holy Spirit says, 'Today, when you hear his voice, do not harden your hearts as in the rebellion' " (3, 7f.). His purpose is to emphasize the "today" of the scriptural quotation, and to evoke a new and immediate zeal. Finally, it is also made clear that God's revealed word, as well as his preached word which takes up the former, approaches man from without and demands an interior decision from him. It is, therefore, in a different manner of speaking—having no bearing on the events of revelation here referred to—that Jesus with a shout of joy gives thanks to the father who has "hidden these things from the wise and understanding and revealed them to babes" (Mt. 11, 25; Lk. 10, 21). This interior, gracious revealing of the Father not only does not make superfluous the external revelation of the Son, but in fact presupposes it.

(h) "... by a Son ..." Eschatological revelation is achieved only through this One: this is emphasized by the lack of the article which is often omitted where "the union is present in only one individual."[9] The Son is not only the last in a long line of revelation mediators, he is also the absolute and unsurpassable culmination and therefore the final and perfect revealer.[10] This is a certainty in the Christological ex-

[9] Blass-Debrunner, *Grammatik des ntl Griechisch,* ninth ed., 1954, §252, 2.

[10] O. Michel: "In contrast to Philo, the thought of the Letter to the Hebrews is historical, messianic, and eschatological."

planation of Heb. 1—2, but it is also the evident conviction of the other New Testament authors. The fact that the Son's revelation maintains a unique, incomparable, exclusive position insofar as it alone effects salvation, also appears in the Gospel of St. John: "No one has ever seen God; the only Son, who is in the bosom of the Father, he has made him known" (1, 18). Another manner of divine revelation, the immediate vision of God, is not granted to man: whoever "sees" the Son also "sees" the Father; whoever believes in the Son possesses not only the Son but also the Father and life eternal (see Jn. 14, 8ff.; 1 Jn. 2, 23; 5, 10ff.). But at the same time, John's words about the Paraclete make it clear that the revelation of Jesus-in-the-world is yet in need of "evocation" and interpretation by the Spirit who is sent by the transfigured Christ, or, more precisely, by the apostles filled with and guided by that same Spirit (see Jn. 14, 26; 16, 12ff.).

If we examine the understanding of New Testament revelation set forth in Heb. 1, 1, the peculiar relationship between biblical revelation and human history becomes clear. Revelation is historical insofar as it is bound to human history—in the Old Testament, especially the history of the chosen people—and yet it transcends historical events insofar as revelation is eternally valid; and, as it culminates in the revelation of the Son, it is definitive and eschatological. It is historical also in terms of its authenticity, in that it exhorts man to decision—man who freely guides his own destiny, who determines his present existence in light of the past and in view of the future. The existential mind asks how eschatological revelation confronts man in his *existence:*[11] whether objective truths can be set before man or whether revelation, that is, the eschatological event itself, does not rather place him in the position of deciding for himself to win or to lose his *actuality.*

Already in 1929, Rudolf Bultmann[12] raised this question in all its acuteness, and answered it in light of his own mode of existential theology. For him, revelation is "nothing other than the fact of Jesus Christ" (p. 18). "Revelation is not an enlightenment, not the communication of information, but a *happening*" (p. 21) of which the proclamation is a part. "The revelation-event is not a cosmic occurrence completed outside of ourselves of which the Word would bring us tidings (meaning that it would be no more than a myth). Revelation, then, must be a happening which affects us directly, which is completed in ourselves—and the Word, the fact itself of the message-being-proclaimed, is an integral part of that occurrence" (*ibid.*). Bultmann finds his interpretation reinforced especially by the Johannine Gospel. "John most strongly emphasizes the paradox: Jesus is sent

[11] See J. B. Metz, "Befindlichkeit," in *Lexikon für Theologie und Kirche,* second ed., II, pp. 102–104; A. Darlapp, "Geschichtlichkeit," in *ibid.,* IV, pp. 780–783; G. Bauer, *Geschichtlichkeit. Wege und Irrwege eines Begriffs,* Berlin, 1963.

[12] "Der Begriff der Offenbarung im Neuen Testament," reprinted in "Glauben und Verstehen," *Ges. Aufsätze,* III, Tübingen, 1960, p. 1–40 (specific page references given in the text of the present book).

as the revealer, and what does he reveal? *The fact that he is sent* as the revealer! This we are told to believe, and from this belief we are asked to draw life . . . Outside of faith, revelation is invisible: nothing is revealed which commands belief. The object of faith is revealed only by faith itself: for this reason faith is a part of revelation" (p. 23). What, therefore, has been revealed? Nothing whatever—if the question as to what revelation teaches refers to teachings which no man could arrive at; to mysteries which, once made known, are known for all time. But, in fact, *everything* has been revealed, insofar as *man's eyes are opened to himself, and he can again understand himself"* (p. 29—Bultmann's emphasis).

We immediately recognize the well-known and much-discussed theses of Bultmann, his hermeneutic approach to man's self-interpretation, his concept of "myth," the demand of the "existential" interpretation, and so forth. At this point we are only interested in his understanding of revelation. Measuring it against Heb. 1, 1f., we may acknowledge his positive desire to see revelation as the message of God (see *ibid.* p. 30); but we may also ask whether this kind of purely existential message corresponds to the New Testament or whether it minimizes and distorts the real meaning of the New Testament message. The Gospel of St. John also says clearly enough—if one does not "demythologize" it of the alleged myth of the Gnostic messenger or reduce its assertions concerning the Son to the significance of his having come—that the believer must admit not only the fact but also the message of the revealer; not only the occurrence but also the content of his revelation; not only the salvific import of his word but also the salvific import of his very person.[13] We may further ask whether Bultmann has not read into the New Testament message a vague, generalized concept of revelation when he includes the message, and faith itself, in revelation.[14] The still unclear terminology may tempt us to ask this, but with careful scrutiny of the matter (again in connection with Heb. 1, 1f.), we will certainly recognize the fact that, of course, revelation reaches the hearer through proclamation; the word of revelation has the power of addressing, of exhorting, in the word of proclamation—and yet it is not totally absorbed by it, but maintains its historical and theological uniqueness. Likewise, faith is indeed man's response to divine revelation, and yet it is not itself a part of the revelation-event: revelation exists validly even where there is no response. Finally, we may ask whether Bultmann even takes into consideration the revela-

[13] For a critique of Bultmann see, among others, Th. Müller, *Das Heilsgeschehen im Johannesevangelium,* Zürich-Frenkfukt a.M. o.J., 1961; J. Blank, *Krisis. Untersuchungen zur joh Christologie und Eschatologie* (unpublished dissertation), Würzburg, 1962.

[14] One might also say that Bultmann's concept of revelation is "narrower," in that for him, revelation consists only in the personal address. Significant for his existential interpretation is the sentence, "[The revelational event is] understood in its actual character only if it is understood *as being accomplished in the present, yes, in my present,*" p. 22. For a critique of this, see J. Brinktrine, "Der Begriff der Offenbarung im Neuen Testament," in *TGl* 34, 1942, pp. 76–83, esp. pp. 81f.

tion-history alluded to in Heb. 1, 1f. Understood existentially, revelation (through the word of proclamation) touches each man in his uniqueness and confronts him with the eschatological decision, but it cannot itself become a history progressing from the self-disclosure of God to the climax of the revelation of the Son.

Old Testament exegetes especially are led by the texts to a judgment different from the existential one: they tend to regard history—that is, the history of the chosen people—as salvation history in and through which revelation takes place. In effect, to them, salvation history is the same thing as revelation history.

Even a few unbiased voices will serve to demonstrate this fact. In an article on this subject, W. Eichrodt writes: "The actuality and the truth of divine revelation is imparted to man, not disjoint from history as timeless, abstract teaching, but rather in, with, and under historical appearance. It will therefore become truly effective only for him who opens himself to its history."[15] M. Noth, after comparison with texts of Mari, remarks: "According to biblical tradition, God encounters man in the midst of the unholy, that is, the not divine world, and for this he makes use of the historical happenings of this world. This becomes very clear from the fundamental content of the New Testament. If it is true that the area of divine activity in the Old Testament is the history

[15] "Offenbarung und Geschichte im Alten Testament," in *TZ Bas* 4, 1948, pp. 321–331; this reference p. 328.

of Israel (so G. Menshing), this means that here—in an occurrence which is in every respect and in relation to the most subtle *Lebensäusserungen* [statements about life] contingent upon history—here is the sphere of efficacy of the word of God."[16] G. von Rad, who only examines the traditions of Israel and considers their testimony to be "vastly various," nevertheless recognizes the common element of the testimony: "They [the Israelite traditions] limit themselves to the representation of only one aspect of the relation between Yahweh and Israel [and the world]: to wit, as a continuing, divine activity in history. This is as much as to say that the faith of Israel is basically historico-theological."[17] Similarly, E. Jacob notes: "What makes biblical revelation so unique is the fact that God unites himself to the events of history in order to make manifest his plan."[18] S. Amsler, in his fine work *The Old Testament and the Church,* speaks of "revelation history" and characterizes the central message of the Old Testament as follows: "The Old Testament bears witness to the living God who has revealed himself to Israel through his intervention on the stage of secular history."[19] M. Burrows explains: "The conviction

[16] "Geschichte und Gotteswort im Alten Testament," in *Gesammelte Studien zum AT,* München, 1957, pp. 230–247; this reference p. 245.

[17] *Theologie des Alten Testaments,* I, München, 1957, p. 112 (see also pp. 120f.).

[18] *Théologie de l'Ancien Testament,* Neuchâtel, 1955, p. 153. See the entire section entitled "Foi et Histoire," pp. 148–163.

[19] *L'Ancien Testament dans l'Eglise,* Neuchâtel, 1960, pp. 108–119; this reference p. 108.

that God is revealed in history and especially in the history of the chosen people explains why there is so much history in the Bible. . . . The special revelation of God given in the history of Israel reaches its culmination in the incarnation of God in Christ."[20] In much the same manner E. G. Wright, in his worthwhile little book *God Who Acts,* demands a comprehensive Old and New Testament biblical theology, and makes the following assertion about God who continually reveals himself in the entire Bible: "The nature of his being and will is revealed in historical acts"; Wright also notes that, in contrast to the prevailing tendency, Jesus does not emphasize "spiritual experience." "The main emphasis of the Bible is certainly on [God's] revelation of himself in historical acts and in definite words, and not in diffuse experience."[21]

The correlation between revelation and salvation history is admitted by numerous scholars, though it is not always judged in like manner. Did God reveal himself (with increasing clearness until the time of Jesus Christ) *in the course of history* (especially the history of the people of Isael), above all in his speaking, in his messages to the mediators of revelation, manifold messages witnessing to his divine plans and deeds, giving guidance and advice until

[20] *An Outline of Biblical Theology,* Philadelphia, 1946, p. 39.
[21] "God Who Acts" (*Studies in Biblical Theology* 8), London, 1952, pp. 21, 23.

the coming of the Son who "bears witness to what he has seen and heard" (Jn. 3, 32)? Or did God reveal himself *through history itself* in all his activity with the Israelites until the resurrection of Jesus as his eschatological act? This alternative may surprise us, used as we are to associating act and revealed word, comprehending only in their significant unity the self-disclosure of God. The question was recently treated in a co-authored publication, *Revelation as History.*[22] Contesting the systematic approach, the editor, W. Pannenberg, speaks of an "indirect self-revelation of God in history" and denies any direct self-communication on God's part.[23] His fundamental thesis is that "God's self-revelation, according to biblical testimony, was accomplished not directly, as in a theophany, but indirectly through God's historical acts" (p. 91). Now, the notions of direct and indirect may be disputed; no one would postulate a direct theophany in the Bible. However, both exegeses (Old Testament: R. Rendtorff; New Testament: U. Wilckens) conceal the revealing God behind his deeds accomplished in history, to the extent that we may wonder whether this still corresponds to the understanding of revelation by the biblical authors (for

[22] *Offenbarung als Geschichte,* R. Rendtorff, U. Wilckens, and T. Rendtorff, edited by W. Pannenberg, Göttingen, 1961.

[23] Pannenberg believes that a direct self-revelation of God cannot be concluded or asserted either from the biblical equivalents for "revealing," or from the concepts of "announcement of the name of God," "word of God," and "proclamation of the law" (*loc. cit.,* pp. 11–16).

which we have already seen Heb. 1, 1f. as a concise summary).

Wilckens comes to the conclusion: "Revelation, in the theological sense in which it is here used, is contained solely in the event of the resurrection from the dead of the crucified Jesus of Nazareth, in which God established the new aeon—this is the unanimous finding of the otherwise so varied testimony of primitive Christianity" (p. 87). Although the resurrection of Jesus is for the early Church so indisputably the seal of the divine revelation achieved in the Son, and at the same time the foreshadowing disclosure of eschatological fulfillment, one can hardly classify the verbal revelation in terms of the resurrection nor subordinate the former to the latter. Wilckens says much of note concerning "revelation in the appearance and destiny of Jesus" (p. 50–63), but he does not see clearly enough the role of Jesus as the only totally empowered revealer. To be sure, the message of Jesus is directly related to the salvific revelation of God ensuing from his destiny so that we might subscribe to the following statement: "There is, rather, a direct path leading from the claim of Jesus himself to the kernel of the primitive Christian belief in the resurrected one" (p. 61). However, we must also acknowledge the importance of Christ's words themselves lest all of revelation be exhausted by the action of God. This suspicion is supported by Pannenberg's seventh thesis: "The word is linked to revelation as prediction, as instruction, and as report" (p. 112). The "words authorized by the God of Israel and Jesus of Nazareth . . . form the context of these events" and perform the functions enumerated in the preceding thesis. Pannenberg emphatically says: "The occurrences by which God has demonstrated his divinity are as such self-evident within their historical context. There is no need for inspired interpretation which only in supplementing the occurrence would make it recognizable as revelation" (pp. 113f.). This sentence refers only to the word of God as kerygma; but by the same token, the word of God as promise and as instruction is stripped of all traces of its original revelational significance.

With this theological view it seems that the emphasis against the dialectic word-theology becomes too strong. God's speaking through the mouths of the prophets and his direct self-revelation in the word and works of his Son; his salvation-history activity with the Israelites and his eschatological intervention in the destiny of his Son (in the resurrection and the ascension) are combined into a complete historico-eschatological revelation. Biased opinions, after all, have a certain validity in that they give (if excessive yet necessary) emphasis to points of note. So in this case, both the desire to understand revelation as "allocution," and the endeavor to perceive God's revelation in his historical deeds, ought to become integrated with our understanding of revelation.

2. REVELATION AND FAITH

Is biblical revelation (we might say manifestation) truly *manifest,* or does it remain in some ways veiled and obscure? Has God made himself so clearly visible in biblical (at least, in New Testament eschatological) revelation, in will and work, in essence and act, in intent towards the salvation of man—has God made himself so clearly and completely visible that man cannot but see and comprehend him and his ways? St. Paul was already concerned with this question, particularly with reference to the effectiveness of his own proclamation, his preaching by which, after all, he made the message of salvation accessible to man. Twice does he seek an answer. In 2 Cor. 4, 3ff., the apostle acknowledges the fact that his preaching is not universally successful, and remarks: "And even if our gospel is veiled, it is veiled only to those who are perishing. In their case the god of this world has blinded the minds of the unbelievers, to keep them from seeing the light of the gospel of the glory of Christ, who is the likeness of God." In very essence, revelation is a flame which ought to illume the heart like that light on the morning of creation which broke forth when God said, "Let light shine out of darkness" (see verse 6). But if revelation does not have this effect, the blame is not to be laid on God and his revelation in Jesus Christ, but on the men themselves upon whom the light falls, but who have lost the faculty to perceive it because Satan has blinded them, who are already doomed. The fact that Paul is not thinking simply of divine reprobation (to which interpretation the expression "ἐν τοῖς ἀπολλυμένοις" might mislead us[24]) is evident from the subsequent "τῶν ἀπίστων" of verse 4, which can only refer to those previously characterized as "ἀπολλυμένοις." Correspondingly, "we" are they whose hearts God has enlightened with his salvific revelation, who *do* believe in the Gospel of the glory of Christ. This is certainly no answer to the question of predestination, but the best answer is surely that revelation must be approached *in faith* if it is to be effective towards salvation.

The second, and no less important instance of Paul's concern with the subject is found in 1 Cor. 1, 18–25. Here, too, Paul sees mankind divided into the saved and the damned; here again he emphasizes the importance of faith as necessary for receptiveness to the revelation message, and for the attainment of salvation (note how this is expressed by the terminal position of "τοὺς πιστεύοντας" in verse 22). Back of this faith, of course, stands the effective call of God ("τοῖς κλητοῖς," verse 24) and, finally, the mystery of predestination. But here, the apostle finds in the *content* of the message the reason why so many close themselves to the preaching of God's salvific revelation: it is the λόγος τοῦ σταυροῦ, that provocative and scandalous message of the cross of Christ

---

[24] The present participle has overtones of futurity (see Blass-Debrunner, §339, 2); in this connection see Cor. 2, 15f. Therefore the translation "among the lost," or even less "among the rejected," is not correct.

which cannot be understood by human reason or by the wisdom of this world. For this is God's message of *folly* to a world which neither understood nor accepted his previous revelation of the truth (see verse 21). This viewpoint further brings to the fore the problem of "revealing revelation": the eschatological revelation of salvation is to our way of thinking sombre and gruesome in its perpetual emphasis on the message of the cross of Christ, and this difficulty is overcome only in the light of the resurrection (see 1 Cor. 2, 8) —but for comprehension *faith* is absolutely necessary.

P. Althaus treats of this subject in a critical lecture[25] refuting Pannenberg's thesis that "historical revelation is clear to all who have eyes to see." Pannenberg attempts to prove that God's historical actions are in themselves strong enough to carry conviction. "Now these events have truly the power to convince. Wherever they are perceived in their true nature, in the historical context proper to them, they speak their own language, the language of fact. . . . Faith is not necessary to him who seeks God's revelation in the history of Israel and of Jesus Christ. It is rather by the frank apperception of these very events that genuine faith is first awakened."[26] The Catholic theologian will not entirely contradict this hypothesis, but will in fact recognize its affinity with his own point of view, for he agrees that "*recta ratio*

[25] "Offenbarung als Geschichte und Glaube," in *TLZ* 87, 1962, pp. 321–330.
[26] Pannenberg, *loc. cit.,* pp. 100f.

fidei fundamenta demonstret,"[27] and speaks of the *"motiva credibilitatis."* But what does it mean to say that genuine faith is first awakened? The relationship between "recognition of revelation" and "faith" is none too clear from Pannenberg's other remarks.[28] On the other hand, Althaus's thesis that the *grace* of faith is necessary for the faithful comprehension of revelation cannot be disputed on the basis of New Testament texts, as was determined by the Second Council of Orange (Denzinger, 178) and by Vatican I (1791). But his expression "revelation as history and faith" may be ambiguous since it gives the impression that faith itself is integral to the revealed event (see above under heading 1). The inter-Protestant debate, which apparently has not shed enough light on the subject, was initiated with a view to demonstrating the retroactivity of revelation-understanding on the interpretation of faith, and its meaning in regard to faith.

Divine revelation is, therefore, "manifest" insofar as God potentially reveals and makes accessible to every man both himself and the revelation of salvation. Yet, in another sense, it remains "hidden" insofar as it is not actually accessible to all men but only to those who believe. The cosmic universal and public nature of New Testament revelation distinguishes it from the private revelation found in apoca-

[27] Vatican I, Session III, Chapter 4 (Denzinger, 1799).
[28] See Pannenberg, *loc. cit.,* p. 102, note 15. There is also some obscurity in his concept of "faith," which he identifies essentially with "trust," and orients in the future (p. 101).

lyptical circles and special groups (for example, Qumrân[29]);
its emphasis on faith which alone can unlock its effectiveness
and its salvific character preserves it from confusion with
humanly perceptible wisdom and philosophies.

This dual character of New Testament revelation explains
many things in our Gospel tradition. Although Jesus announced his message of salvation openly before all people,
only a very few grasped the true meaning of his revelation,
the eschatological dawn of God's dominion in his activity
and in his person; indeed only they grasped it to whom "has
been given the secret of the kingdom of God" (Mk. 4, 11),
the "babes" to whom the Father has revealed these things
(see Mt. 11, 25; Lk. 10, 21). By the same token, any tension
between the Gospels of St. Mark and St. John can be ex-
plained. It used to be thought that as in the synoptics the
significance of revelation lies in its obscurity, so in the fourth
Gospel it lies its in radiant openness.[30] But the secret of the
Messiah in St. Mark, less pronounced with the other two

[29] See P. Volz, *Die Eschatologie der jüdischen Gemeinde im neutes-
tamentlichen Zeitalter,* Tübingen, 1934, pp. 4f.; A. Oepke in *TWNT* III,
pp. 580f. With reference to Qumrân, see O. Betz, *Offenbarung und
Schriftforschung in der Qumrânsekte,* Tübingen, 1960. The attitude of
Qumrân (is there a "present prophecy," or would that merely be the interpretation of the old scriptural prophecy?) is not uniformly judged: compare,
for example, the opinion of R. Meyer in *TWNT* VI, p. 821, with that of
J. Hempel, *Die Texte von Qumrân in der heutigen Forschung* (special
edition, taken from *Nachr. der Akademie der Wiss. in Göttingen*),
Göttingen, 1962, p. 349; between these two opinions stands that of Betz,
loc. cit., pp. 98f.

[30] H. H. Huber, *Der Begriff der Offenbarung im Johannesevangelium,*
Göttingen, 1934, p. 79.

synoptic writers, has more profound reasons—certainly more than one. Historically speaking, it attests to the fact that the revelation of Jesus was subject to misjudgment and abuse by reason of the worldly, incredulous attitude of the common people; Christologically speaking, it points up the humility of the Son of man who was not understood, even by the most intimate of his disciples, and was forced to walk alone the way to his death on the cross. But, speaking in terms of the theology of revelation, it should become clear to the faithful that only after Easter—in the light of his resurrection—can the revelation of Jesus fully be understood (see Mk. 9, 9). In any case, the resurrection illumines the uniqueness of Jesus' messianic self-witness and of his salvific revelation, which were indeed patent in his healing, his driving out of devils, but which wanted believing eyes and ears. Basically, the fourth Gospel bears witness to the same point, if with a different theological orientation. With his pronounced Christological point of view, the fourth evangelist emphasizes the fact that the eschatological, salvific revelation of God is fully present in the word and deed of Jesus because he is the Messiah in an unanticipated and unsuspected sense—the only-begotten Son of God, the Son of man who truly came down from heaven. At the same time, it becomes evident that "open" revelation is "open" only to those who believe (see 18, 20). Only for them have his works become signs pregnant with revelation (see 2, 11; 6, 26; 9, 38f.; 11, 25ff., 40; 20, 30f.)—for the others they remain the miraculous signs (see 2, 23; 6, 2. 14 etc.) which are constantly being demanded but which, with all their drama, are unable to lead to faith (12, 37). Only for the faithful have his revealed words become "spirit and life" (compare 6, 63[b] with 68[b].)—while for the others they are not "public" enough (see 10, 24f.; also 7, 3ff.) but become rather a cause of scandal and malicious disbelief (see 6, 61; 8, 45ff., 59; 10, 37ff.; 15, 22ff.). Only the faithful have seen the glory of the incarnate Logos revealed in word and in sign (1, 14), and only the faithful will henceforth realize and accept unto their own salvation the historico-eschatological revelation of Christ which is present for them in the word of revelation, and indeed even in this Gospel (see 17, 20; 20, 31; 1 Jn 1, 1–3). Mark therefore shows—alongside the obscured messianic mystery—a revelation which is utterly accessible, if only after the resurrection of Jesus. John, on the other hand—alongside the radiant revelation in the public testimony of Jesus—shows a far more profoundly effective mystery. To be sure, everything is here open, pronounced: the mystery remains because of the disbelief of the world[31]; the word of the divine revealer, no matter how patent, is not patent to human insight, but only to those whom the Father chooses (see 6, 44).

The above has certain implications with regard to faith—faith in terms of man's conduct in response to divine revelation. In this particular theological sense, faith is something

[31] H. Schulte, *loc. cit.,* p. 19.

other than mere natural awareness, acquiescence, knowledge, trust, or hope—no matter how much spiritual energy those activities may in themselves consume. The Catholic conception of faith all too often overlooks the fact that, with all the *motiva credibilitatis* at the disposal of reason, faith itself is still a supernatural virtue *"qua, Dei aspirante et adiuvante gratia, ab eo revelata vera esse credimus."* By emphasizing the utter dependence of man on God as Creator and Lord,[32] and by urging us to extend to the revealing God, in faith, our perfect obedience of reason and will—by these instructions, Vatican I also alludes to the personal union of the faithful with the revealing God, that is to say, with Christ, in whom God reveals himself.[33] Thus faith becomes the existential attitude of man in the state of grace, man living in Christ—even should the communal life with Christ and God be disturbed by sin. Now if faith is emphasized as a total personal commitment to God, it would perhaps be profitable to amend our understanding of the concept of "faith" from the usual one. For this, an examination of what the Bible has to say about faith will be especially helpful.[34]

[32] Session III, Chapter 3 (Denzinger, 1789).

[33] *Ibid.: "Cum homo a Deo tamquam creatore et Domino suo totus dependeat et ratio creata increatae Veritati penitus subiecta sit, plenum revelanti Deo intellectus et voluntatis obsequium fide praestare tenemur."*

[34] See R. Schnackenburg, "Glauben nach den Aussagen der Bibel," in *Glauben heute,* edited by J. M. Reuss, Mainz, 1962, pp. 13–35. The compatibility of the conception prevalent today—that faith is essentially the personal surrender of the whole man to the self-revealing God—with the teaching of Vatican I points to J. M. Reuss, "Der Glaube als komplexer Akt," *ibid.,* pp. 156–167.

3. REVELATION IN WRITTEN AND ORAL TRADITION

It is remarkable that divine revelation, which initially was effected orally—or, as in the case of historical deeds and events, found tangible expression in the word of the mediator of revelation—that this revelation should subsequently have been historified, recorded in sacred Scripture, and this not by way of a purely human undertaking, not for the purpose of retaining the fleeting word and committing it to memory, but at the instigation of God and with his assistance. This is the conviction both of Jesus with regard to the Old Testament, and of the Church with regard to the New. In the same way, the word of the divine revealer came to us, and together with the word came the Logos himself—the Way and the Life—and was made permanently present to us in a particular manner (see Jn. 8, 31; 12, 48; 15, 7). If the human language used by God in revelation is in itself a "gracious condescension" of God—comparable to the incarnation of the Logos himself[35]—how much more gracious is the embodiment of the word of God in Scripture. This brings us to a theological problem, a notable one in light of the Protestant-Catholic controversy on Scripture-versus-tradi-

[35] Proceeding from St. John Chrysostom's teaching on the συγκατάβασις of God in biblical revelation, Pius XII says in the encyclical *Divino afflante Spiritu*: "*Sicut enim substantiale Dei Verbum hominibus simile factum est quoad omnia 'absque peccato'* (Heb. 4, 15), *ita etiam Dei verba, humanis linguis expressa, quoad omnia humano sermoni assimilia facta sunt, excepto errore*" (*Enchiridion Biblicum*, Rome, second ed., 1954, no. 559).

tion: What is the relation between "oral revelation" and the inspired scriptural orientation of the Bible? It will be impossible here to enter into an exhaustive discussion of the whole complex of questions involved, particularly since the actual question—whether there exists, in addition to the apostolic tradition recorded in the New Testament, a tradition transmitted only orally, if with apostolic warranty (tradition in the narrower sense)—cannot be answered directly and conclusively on New Testament evidence.[36] However, we may exegetically adduce certain points of view of no little significance in this matter of the relationship between written and oral tradition.

First of all, there is a certain analogy (but no more!) between the position of the primitive Church on Old Testament Scripture and the oral apostolic tradition on the one hand, and the position of the Church today on New Testament Scripture and its subsequent tradition. In the use of the Old Testament, the early Church by no means limited herself to the material that could be perceived directly in divine revelation and in Scripture.

It will immediately be objected that, for the early Church, the interpretation and the continuing revelation of Jesus Christ were novel and authoritative, so that she found herself in a totally new revelational situation. It is obvious, however, that in using the Old Testament, she not only adhered

---

[36] See M. Schmaus, *Katholische Dogmatik* I, 1, München, third and fourth eds., 1948, pp. 116–118.

strictly to the mandatory word of God, but also of herself went beyond it. Her Christological interpretation of the Old Testament may certainly be seen as the development of the Christic revelation, which after all does not consist alone of the word of the man Jesus, but includes the events of his resurrection and ascension as well. But how is it that Paul feels free, for example, to set forth such a radical "typological" interpretation in 1 Cor. 10, 1–11, in which he even adopts certain post-biblical Hebrew theologoumena translated into Christian terms? He allows himself to be led by his faith in Christ, confident in the guidance of the power of the Holy Spirit (see 1 Cor. 7, 40). In this way, there grew up a tradition which transcended the written word of God of the Old Testament and the spoken Gospel concerning Jesus Christ (as well as the words of Jesus himself up to that point)—a tradition which was in no wise contradictory to previous revelation while at the same time adding considerable new matter (for example, the Old Testament "τύποι" corresponds to the New Testament sacraments), as Paul is well aware.[37]

It must again be stressed that we are here dealing only with an analogy to the "oral apostolic tradition," for St. Paul's exegesis has meanwhile, of course, come to be regarded as a part of scriptural tradition (and as the inspired

---

[37] See the introductory phrase "οὐ θέλω γὰρ ὑμᾶς ἀγνοεῖν" (1 Cor. 10, 1), which is also used elswhere when St. Paul draws the attention of his readers to some new thing (1 Thess. 4, 13; Rom. 11, 25; 2 Cor. 1, 8).

word of God). St. Paul's preaching was for the most part verbal, however, and we may wonder how much of it has (accidentally) failed to be transmitted to us through his letters. On the other hand, we may herein discern the function of verbal apostolic preaching vis-à-vis the revelation at hand: its primary purpose is *interpretation,* the clarification and more thorough development of divine revelation as recorded in Scripture, a fully authorized interpretation made under the guidance of the Holy Spirit on the basis of Christ's eschatological revelation. Basically, this interpretation includes nothing new, nothing beyond that revelation, and yet it appears as new by contrast with the "historical" documents of the Old Testament and also in view of the explicitly formulated revelation of Jesus Christ and of his Gospel.

A second, even more apropos example of the relationship between written and oral tradition is to be found in the *Gospel tradition.* It hardly suffices to point out that oral tradition existed before the written and is therefore in a position of eminence not forfeited even to the subsequent written tradition. At the same time, it is of fundamental import to discover that each of our Gospels attempts to present the salvation message of Jesus Christ as an independent whole, and yet does not report in detail the entirety of Jesus' revelation. This is particularly true in the case of St. Mark's Gospel, for how else are we to understand the "headline" "ἀρχὴ τοῦ εὐαγγελίου Ἰησοῦ Χριστοῦ" (1, 1) than as the

121

pronouncement that in the subsequent writing the essential portions of Jesus Christ's salvation message are to be revealed? And yet this fails to report not only a good number of events which we might consider superfluous to the decisive revelation of the way of salvation opened to us by God through Christ, but in fact fails to report even such important scenes as the sermon on the mount, or the conferral of primacy on Simon Peter. Of course, we may simply assert that it was the will of God to give us as scriptural treasure and source of revelation not only the Gospel of St. Mark, but also the other three. And yet, there must have been communities who initially had only the Gospel of St. Mark containing the essential parts, but not the entirety of the apostolic preaching; and it is scarcely conceivable that these communities should have rejected any apostolic word from other, verbal sources as long as they were well-founded. This situation is even more palpable in the case of the fourth Gospel. Here the evangelist is aware that he presents only a selection of the σημεῖα of Jesus (20, 30), and yet it is the very purpose of his Gospel to make possible to his readers the salvific belief in Jesus, the Messiah, the Son of God (20, 31), obviously without need of supplement by the other Gospels. Here again, were there not communities who in the beginning had only the Gospel of St. John, and therefore did not possess all of the apostolic tradition?

The Gospel of St. John clarifies in yet another way the relationship between written and oral tradition. So far from

minimizing the importance of the preaching of revelation—
that is, of the oral transmission of revelation—with its recording of the revelation of Christ in Scripture, it in fact
opens the way to future oral revelation. For it speaks not
only of those who will believe in Christ through the word
of the apostles (17, 20), but promises to the disciples of
Jesus the assistance of the Paraclete, who will remind them
of all that Jesus had told them (14, 26), and who will be the
one to lead them to the fullness of wisdom—so that they
may comprehend those things which Jesus at the time of his
life on earth could not make completely clear to them[38]
(see 16, 12f.). Now we may object that it is this very office
of the Paraclete which is evident in the fourth Gospel:
even its form attests to the apostolic interpretation of Christic
revelation made possible by the Paraclete. But does the
evangelist intend to show, by this recording, this finalization,
so to speak, that the work of the Paraclete has been completed? According to 14, 16, this assistance is promised to
the disciples until eternity. No matter how we interpret this
promise to the disciples (as referring to them personally,
or to them as representatives of the community of the faithful), there is nothing to indicate that the recorded Gospel
is meant to be the "boundary" of the activity of the Paraclete.
This book of the Gospel purposes to present to its readers
the revelation of Christ in the light of sanctified (spirit-

[38] See F. Mussner, "Die johanneischen Parakletsprüche und die apostol-
ische Tradition," in BZ NF 5, 1961, pp. 56–70.

filled), reliable apostolic interpretation, but does not exclude other apostolic traditions or subsequent interpretations based on the latter. But that the first preaching of the apostles (in its entirety) forms the definitive foundation for the faith is confirmed by the First Letter of St. John, with its continual reference to those things which the readers have heard "from the beginning" (2, 7. 24; 3, 11).

O. Cullmann theorizes that with the setting up of the Canon the Church has made an "act of humility" by which she "subjects every tradition proceeding from out of herself to the yardstick of the apostolic tradition embedded in holy Scripture."[39] But would it not be more accurate to say, according to the analogy of the Gospel of St. John, that the Church at that time determined positively that the apostolic tradition is contained clearly and reliably in the canonical (inspired) Scriptures, but that it is not contained *only* in them? For her purpose then was to remove all doubts in regard to the *Scriptures* contained in the Canon (as is also evident from the formulations of the Council), but not to make any judgment as to the (oral) tradition living in herself. In this way she neither waived the right to further supervise the correct interpretation of the revelation contained in the Bible and guaranteed by God himself, nor did she make any pronouncement with regard to the apostolic tradition coming to her outside of the Bible, possibly orally.

[39] *Die Tradition als exegetisches, historisches und theologisches Problem,* Zürich, 1954, p. 45.

Should we not then interpret her decision of that time not as an act of humility, but rather as an assertion of her sovereignty born out of the conviction that the Holy Spirit is granted her to recognize and determine the truth in controversial questions?

As to the newer Catholic controversy, whether revelation is contained *partim-partim* or *et-et* in Scripture and in oral tradition,[40] the exegete will, in view of the above analogy from the New Testament context, more readily lean towards the idea that the principal function of tradition is to open up, to develop the interpretation of holy Scripture, without attempting to give a competent answer to this question which goes beyond the New Testament. But since St. Paul hardly adds anything *essentially* new to the apostolic tradition before him, and since each of the evangelists presents what he feels to be the essential portion of the revelation of Christ, we may assume that oral tradition, in the narrower sense, bears the same basic relation to written revelation inspired by God.[41] Most significantly, however, the New

[40] For a discussion of this question see P. Lengsfeld, *Ueberlieferung*, Paderborn, 1960, pp. 118–128; J. R. Geiselmann, *Die Heilige Schrift und die Tradition* (*Quaestiones Disputatae* 18), Freiburg i. Br., 1962; G. Moran, *Scripture and Tradition. A Survey of the Controversy*, New York, 1963.

[41] The interpretation of the Fathers, too, points in this direction. See the opinions quoted by Lengsfeld, *loc. cit.*, pp. 120f. St. Augustine, for example, clearly states: *"In iis enim quae aperte in Scripturis posita sunt, inveniuntur illa omnia quae continent fidem, moresque vivendi, spem scilicet atque caritatem"* (*De doctr. chr.*, II, 9; PL 34, 42). The same is taught by the great medieval theologians and by many contemporary ones; thus P. Lengsfeld says "Every Catholic theologian can subscribe to

Testament focuses on the *unity* of divine revelation, whether with reference to the word of God revealed "once to the fathers through the prophets" and "spoken in these latter days to us in the Son," that is, with reference to the Old and New Testaments; or to the oral preaching of the apostles and their kerygma recorded in writing (see 2 Thess. 2, 15). Nor does the Church wish us to understand "Scripture" and "tradition" other than as springs which both bear witness to one and the same divine revelation and therefore flow into one stream.

---

the view of early-Church and medieval doctrinal tradition that the entire truth of salvation is contained in Scripture" (*loc. cit.,* p. 120). Tradition as a secondary source of revelation is not thereby devaluated or made superfluous. It remains necessary for a guarantee (inspiration and canon), for decisive interpretation, for the deciphering and development of the scriptural word of God, and demonstrates—especially where it is mainly used not as a supplement to content, but for enlightenment and deepening of understanding—its harmony with holy Scripture.